Security *and* Development *in* India's Northeast

Security *and* Development *in* India's Northeast

GURUDAS DAS

OXFORD
UNIVERSITY PRESS

Oxford University Press is a department of the University of Oxford. It furthers the University's objective of excellence in research, scholarship, and education by publishing worldwide in. Oxford is a registered trademark of Oxford University Press in the UK and in certain other countries

Published in India by
Oxford University Press
YMCA Library Building, 1 Jai Singh Road, New Delhi 110 001, India

First Edition published in 2012

ISBN-13: 978-0-19-807978-1
ISBN-10: 0-19-807978-8

Typeset in Adobe Jenson Pro 11/13.5
by BeSpoke Integrated Solutions, Puducherry, India 605 008

For
Professor Bani Prasanna Misra
who ignited our minds to see things beyond the boundaries

Contents

Tables

Acknowledgements

The present study was conceived in 2000 while I was with Omeo Kumar Das Institute of Social Change and Development (OKDISCD) for a short stint. I am grateful to Professor Atul Goswami, Director of the Institute who has given me an opportunity and academic freedom to work on this project. My only grief is that he is no more with us to see the completion of the work after a decade. I am thankful to Professor A.N.S. Ahmed, Professor Indranee Dutta, Professor Bhupen Sharmah, and Dr Kalyan Das, my colleagues at the Institute, for all their assistance and the excellent academic environment that helped me in conceiving the work. I am also thankful to Professor Amalendu Guha, Professor J.B. Ganguly, and Professor Homeswar Goswami for their comments on the draft of the first two chapters, which were presented in an in-house interactive session in the Institute in August 2001.

Later, in 2004, I got some financial assistance from the Indian Council of Social Science Research (ICSSR), New Delhi, to work on the unfinished part of the study. I am particularly thankful to Dr C.J. Thomas, Director, ICSSR–North-Eastern Regional Centre (NERC), for his unstinted support all through the execution of this project. I am also thankful to K. Gyanendra Singh, who has worked as research investigator and collected much of the data that have gone into the making of this study. My colleagues, scholars, and students at the Department of Economics, North-Eastern Hill University (NEHU), Shillong, deserve special thanks for sharing their insights on the society and polity of the Northeastern Region (NER). As I moved from NEHU to the National Institute of Technology (NIT), Silchar, at the end of 2005, the work on the project was delayed. Dr Ashim Kumar Das and Dr N. Bhupendro Singh, my colleagues at NIT, have been a solid support in my academic endeavour for which I shall remain grateful. At the final stage, Debabrata Sutradhar and

Pallabi Das, scholars at the Department of Humanities and Social Sciences, NIT, Silchar, helped me with the structural arrangement of the text and proofreading for which I am thankful to them.

I am also thankful to Gajendra Debchoudhury of OKDISCD library, C. Khongla of ICSSR–NERC library, Pradip Mitra of NEHU library, Eugenia Dimant of Widener library, Harvard University, Kenneth Krompinger of Herbert Lehman library, Mayank Yadav of Columbia University, Dr Sreeradha Datta of Institute for Defence Studies and Analyses, and Dr Prabir De of Research and Information System for Developing Countries (RIS) for giving me access to libraries and providing me with material whenever requested.

I acknowledge with great pleasure the contribution of my wife, Bela, my son, Tamoghna, and my sister-in-law, Malabika, in easing out my life during times of stress and strain, and supporting my endeavour with all their might.

1 August 2011

NIT, Silchar

Gurudas Das

Abbreviations

AASU	All Assam Students Union
ADC	Autonomous District Council
AFSPA	Armed Forces Special Powers Act
AGP	Asom Gana Parishad
AI–FTA	ASEAN–India FTA
AL	Awami League
ALMA	A'chik Liberation Matgrik Army
AMRTDMWU	All Manipur Road Transport Drivers and Motor Workers' Union
ANVC	Achik National Volunteer Council
APCC	Assam Pradesh Congress Committee
APEC	Asia Pacific Economic Cooperation
APHLC	All Party Hill Leaders Conference
ARF	ASEAN Regional Forum
ASEAN	Association of South East Asian Nations
ASEM	Asia–Europe Meeting
ATPLO	All Tripura People's Liberation Organization
ATTF	All Tripura Tribal Force
AXX	Assam Xahitya Xabha
BBIN-GQ	Bangladesh, Bhutan, India, and Nepal-Growth Quadrangle
BdSF	Bodo Security Force
BIMSTEC	Bay of Bengal Initiative for Multi-Sectoral Technical and Economic Cooperation
BPO	Business Process Outsourcing
BSF	Border Security Force
BTC	Bodoland Territorial Council
CAG	Comptroller and Auditor General
CBM	Confidence Building Measure

CBO	Community-based Organization
C-DAC	Centre for the Development of Advanced Computing
CEA	Central Electricity Authority
CECA	Comprehensive Economic Cooperation Agreement
CENTO	Central Treaty Organization
CEPA	Comprehensive Economic Partnership Agreement
CIA	Central Intelligence Agency
CMS	Centre for Media Studies
CPI(M)	Communist Party of India (Marxist)
DHD	Dima Halim Daogah
DNSF	Dimasa National Security Force
DNV	Dimasa National Volunteers
DPIP	Department of Industrial Policy & Promotion
EEZ	Exclusive Economic Zone
EHP	Early Harvest Programme
EHS	Early Harvest Scheme
EITU	Eastern India Tribal Union
EMI	Equal Monthly Instalment
EU	European Union
FDI	Foreign Direct Investment
FGN	Federal Government of Nagaland
FRIDE	Fundación para las Relaciones Internacionales y el Diálogo Exterior
FTA	Free Trade Area
GAIL	Gas Authority of India Ltd
GDP	Gross Domestic Product
GLO	Gorkha Liberation Organisation
GoI	Government of India
GPRN	Government of Peoples' Republic of Nagaland
GSDP	Gross State Domestic Product
HNLC	Hynniewtrep National Liberation Council
HPC	Hmar People's Convention
HPC-D	Hmar People's Convention (Democratic)
IB	Intelligence Bureau
ICSSR	Indian Council of Social Science Research
IDMC	Internal Displacement Monitoring Centre

IDP	Internally Displaced Person
IDSA	Institute for Defence Studies and Analyses
IMCEITS	Indo-Myanmar Centre for Enhancement of IT Skills
IPR	Intellectual Property Right
ISI	Inter-Services Intelligence
ITA	Integration through Assam
JSG	Joint Study Group
KIO	Kachin Independence Organization
KLO	Kamatapur Liberation Organisation
KNA	Kuki National Army
KNV	Karbi National Volunteers
KYKL	Kanglei Yawol Kanna Lup
LAC	Line of Actual Control
LIW	Land Lijke India War Group
LTTE	Liberation Tigers of Tamil Eelam
MCC	Maoist Communist Centre
MEA	Ministry of External Affairs
MGI	Mekong–Ganga Initiative
MHA	Ministry of Home Affairs
MICELT	Myanmar-India Centre for English Language Training
MIEDC	Myanmar-India Entrepreneurship Development Centre
MLA	Muslim Liberation Army
MNF	Mizo National Front
MOD	Ministry of Defence
MOS	Memorandum of Settlement
MoU	Memorandum of Understanding
MSCA	Muslim Security Council of Assam
MSF	Muslim Security Force
MTF	Muslim Tiger Force
MULFA	Muslim United Liberation Front of Assam
MULTA	Muslim United Liberation Tigers of Assam
MVF	Muslim Volunteer Force
NAFTA	North American Free Trade Agreement
NCIP	Netherlands Council on Indigenous People
NDFB	National Democratic Front of Bodoland
NEC	North-Eastern Council

NEFA	North-East Frontier Agency
NEHU	North-Eastern Hill University
NER	Northeastern Region
NERC	North-Eastern Regional Centre
NGO	Non-governmental Organization
NHTA	Naga Hills–Tuensang Area
NIT	National Institute of Technology
NLFT	National Liberation Front of Tripura
NNC	Naga National Council
NNO	Naga Nationalist Organization
NPC	Naga People's Convention
NSCN	National Socialist Council of Nagaland
NSCN (I-M)	National Socialist Council of Nagaland (Isaac-Muivah)
NSCN (K)	National Socialist Council of Nagaland (Khaplang)
NSCN	National Socialist Council of Nagaland
ODA	Official Development Assistance
OECD	Organisation for Economic Co-operation and Development
OKDISCD	Omeo Kumar Das Institute of Social Change and Development
PDS	Public Distribution System
PLA	Peoples' Liberation Army
PLF–M	People's Liberation Front of Meghalaya
PREPAK	People's Revolutionary Party of Kangleipak
PULF	People's United Liberation Front
PWG	People's War Group
RAW	Research and Analysis Wing
RIMS	Regional Institute of Medical Sciences
RIS	Research and Information System for Developing Countries
RTIA	Regional Trade and Investment Area
SAARC	South Asian Association for Regional Cooperation
SAFTA	South Asian Free Trade Area
SAPTA	SAARC Preferential Trading Arrangement
SAWTEE	South Asia Watch on Trade, Economics & Environment

SEATO	South East Asia Treaty Organization
SORO	Special Operations Research Office
SPDC	State Peace and Development Council
SULFA	Surrendered United Liberation Front of Assam
TAR	Tibet Autonomous Region
TNC	Trade Negotiating Committee
TNV	Tripura National Volunteers
TTDF	Tripura Tribal Development Force
TTVF	Tripura Tribal Volunteer Force
TUJS	Tripura Upajati Juba Samiti
TYF	Tribal Youth Force
UBLF	United Bengali Liberation Force
UK	United Kingdom
ULFA	United Liberation Front of Assam
ULFS	United Liberation Front of the Seven Sisters
ULMA	United Liberation Militia of Assam
UMFO	United Mizo Freedom Organization
UMLFA	United Muslim Liberation Front of Assam
UNDP	United Nations Development Programme
UNLF	United National Liberation Front
UPDS	United People's Democratic Solidarity
USSR	Union of Soviet Socialist Republics
WANA	West Asia and North Africa

Introduction

The Need for Dovetailing Security and Development Policies

Security and development has not yet been established as a separate branch of study, although both security and development are quite old as separate branches of pedagogy. For long, security studies have focused primarily on military security from external forces which is essentially state-centric. While security perception of the States is largely rooted in the doctrine of balance of power—global, regional, or local—and dynamics of international relations, the development discourse is fixated strictly within the national framework. However, with the reduction of inter-State wars in post-World War II scenario and the rise in civil wars in poor and less-developed countries in Africa, Asia, and Latin America, it is increasingly realized, mainly at the policy circles, that the perspectives of both the branches need to be harmonized in order to integrate the security and development policies. The contemporary debate on the securitization of development policy or developmentalization of security policy takes its cue from such growing realization about the interdependence between security and development.

Security and development are intricately related. A secure environment promotes development and development, in turn, reduces threat to security. Economic underdevelopment breeds conflict and violence as it provides limited livelihood opportunities to people and denies basic human needs. Similarly, insecurity negatively affects economic development as it raises the level of risks for investment and encourages flight of capital. Thus, insecurity and underdevelopment are both cause and consequence to each other.

Recurring violence is the major source of insecurity in many developing countries of the world. The triggers of conflict are many. Each conflict evolves in a particular social dynamics and hence there is no one-size-fits-all solution for them. Although causes of conflict are different, the consequences are similar—human suffering. It is thus important to delineate the drivers of conflict and recurring violence, and the dynamics of their interlinkages in a particular case to fathom a best-fit strategy for its resolution.

Drivers of Violence

The literature on conflict studies has identified a number of structural factors that increase the risk of violence. Economic underdevelopment is found to be positively correlated with the risk of conflict. Countries with low per capita Gross Domestic Product (GDP) are found to face higher risk compared to countries with higher per capita GDP (Tschirgi *et al.* 2010). Economic underdevelopment means fewer opportunities available for decent livelihood and low opportunity cost for engaging in violence (Collier 2007). Much of the conflict-prone areas and civil-war zones are located in the poor countries and regions that indicate some sort of association between economic underdevelopment and risk of conflict. Besides low income, economic shocks arising from factors beyond the control of a state, like food and energy price shocks, can also raise the risk of conflict (World Bank 2011).

Horizontal inequality between identity groups—ethnic, caste, or religious—is another powerful driver of conflict. Such inequalities may arise due to unequal access to political, economic, or social opportunities. In a multiethnic society characterized by a major ethnic group sharing the socio-political space with a number of smaller ethnic groups, minorities might suffer from perceived or real discriminations. This gives rise to a sense of relative deprivation among the minorities leading to interethnic schism and conflict. Minorities often seek separation projecting their distinct identities as they can only assume the place of majority in a newly carved-out separate political unit.

Resource curse hypothesis (Sachs and Warner 1995) also explains an important cause of conflict in resource-abundant countries. It has been found that economic growth in resource-abundant countries is sluggish compared to resource-scarce countries. This sluggish growth exacerbates conflict. In fact, natural resource occurrence triggers conflict in different ways. Resource ownership often acts as a source of conflict. As resource deposits occur in certain places, people residing in those areas might stake a claim of ownership and oppose the central government to extract it for the benefit of the elite. Rebel leadership might mobilize people based on ethnic identity and demand for secession. Suppression of this demand by the central government then would lead to conflict and violence. Rebel groups might capture and control resources which provide them the sustenance to carry out their rebellion leading to resource war. The greed hypothesis (Collier and Hoeffler 2004) views the greedy behaviour of the rebel groups for the appropriation of resource rents as the cause of conflict. Moreover, resource rents might be used to practice the politics of patronage rather than politics of performance by the elite who appropriate the resource revenue. This will in turn undermine the values of democracy and lead to factional war (Collier 2007).

Inter-group competition for state privileges often acts as the springboard of conflict. Identity groups often compete with each other for a share of government jobs and other privileges like government contracts, trade licences, supply orders, and other pecuniary benefits. Besides public privileges, groups also often compete for land, water, forest, and other natural resources. This competition for public and private resources often leads to inter-group rivalries resulting in conflict and violence (Das 1996; Menkhaus 2010).

Identity and ethnicity are powerful drivers of conflict. An identity group can, in retrospect, question the historical or political process of integration of their homeland with a federal state and assert their identity to claim secession without making any reference to horizontal inequality. Identity may be constructed by the elite of a group for claiming measures of positive discrimination in a federal structure. Ethnocentric behaviour of a group often encourages others to reconstruct their identities. The politics of identity then results into inter-group conflicts which might lead to ethnic cleansing or genocide. Clan cleavages are also found to be a potential source of conflict (Menkhaus 2010).

The youth bulge hypothesis (Cincotta 2010) suggests that countries having large proportion of youth in their population structures tend to have higher risk of conflict. Existence of youth bulge amplifies the inherent tensions that prevail in a society. Youth bulge societies burdened with educated, unemployed youth bear a higher risk of conflict as the young adults are easily attracted by rebel groups and criminal gangs. Youth bulge societies characterized by horizontal inequalities face greater challenges in maintaining social harmony as the youth in minority communities tend to take a lead role in conflicts seeking social justice.

Corruption is another important driver for escalating social conflict, and is responsible for low economic growth, high income inequality and poverty, and lower level of human development (Akcay 2006). It undermines the state's legitimacy and, in extreme cases, may render a country ungovernable and lead to political instability, chaos or war (Bottelier 1998). Rent-seeking behaviour of the elite makes the institutional structure of a country dysfunctional. The frustration among the people in general and the youth in particular who find it difficult to advance their careers in a corrupt environment may join the rebel movements who vow to eliminate it by overthrowing the existing regime.

State oppression and human-rights abuse also acts as triggers for conflict. The direct and indirect victims of state oppression can be easily mobilized by the rebel groups against the state. Moreover, state oppression creates an environment where acts of violence by the opposing forces receive public sympathy. Extrajudicial killing, arbitrary detention, torture, false accusations by the law enforcing agencies, suppression of the freedom of press—all increase the risk of violence. A strong statistical correlation is found between past human-rights abuses and current risk of conflict (World Bank 2011).

Existence of large-scale unemployment is another driver that increases the risk of conflict in a society. Youth who do not find opportunities for living a descent life become frustrated and readily agree to join the rebellion. As the opportunity cost of joining a rebellion is almost negligible, it at least provides them with a certain identity and purpose in life. While the policy circles recognize the problem of unemployment as one of the basic causes of conflict and violence, academics are yet to establish the direction of causation between these two (World Bank 2011).

Weak institutions increase the risk of violence. Societies which lack in well-defined rules, regulations, customs, and norms to govern human behaviour, or even if the regulatory framework is merely there on paper, but not executed or executed only selectively, conflict resolution in such an environment becomes problematic. It has been observed that States with weak institutions run the greatest risk of the onset and recurrence of violence (World Bank 2011).

The psychology of relative deprivation—a feeling of deprivation due to the difference between expectation and attainment—is a powerful driver of conflict and violence (Gurr 1970). A collectivity may compare its socio-economic status with another within the same state and feel deprived. The level of expectation of people rises with educational attainment, but if there are no sufficient job opportunities, people may get frustrated and indulge into violent political movements to press forward their demand. This psychology often becomes stronger where horizontal inequality exists. The intensity of the conflict is determined, to a significant extent, by the degree of perception of the feeling of deprivation among the members of a collectivity.

Polarization of identity is found to act as a significant explanatory variable for civil-war onset (Montalvo and Reynal–Querol 2005). Polarization leads to alienation of ethnic groups and cements binding within the groups (Murshed and Tadjoeddin 2007). As polarization leaves little commonly shared spaces, the scope for negotiated settlement is reduced. Groups having conflicting interests may harden their position leading to conflict and violence.

Failure of democratic conflict-resolution mechanisms is another source of violence. In a parliamentary democracy, political parties articulate the grievances of various segments of the people. Non-fulfilment of aspirations under a particular regime may lead to a change in regime facilitating new initiative towards their resolution. This happens through elections. An electorate may choose a different political party or a combination of forces, which they think will serve their interest better. This is why elections in democracy is often referred to as a silent revolution. However, this built-in conflict resolution mechanism in a democratic process is largely biased in favour of the majority group in a polyethnic society. The smaller communities, not being in a position to influence the outcome of a political verdict, attracts less attention from the competing political parties. The minorities, who are left in a political vacuum, transform themselves into political communities and adopt violence as a political mode of communication (Das 2005a).

Ideology is also one of the powerful drivers of conflict and violence. However, ideology-based conflicts often cut across narrow identities relating to ethnicity or racism or clannish perspectives and seek to effect social transformation for the welfare of the people of a State.

Besides these drivers, external support to rebel groups in a country often helps conflict to linger for a long period causing recurrence of violence. Hostile governments often provide logistics to rebel groups in their fight against the government they oppose. Reciprocal support from hostile neighbours keeps insurgent groups afloat. In many cases, with the involvement of hostile powers, rebel groups in fact wage a proxy war. Once the support structure is withdrawn, such rebellions might collapse (Collier *et al.* 2003). Besides the external governments, diaspora also often plays an important role in supporting conflict as well as in building peace in the country of their origin. Remittances from diaspora are often used for initiating, fomenting, or renewing conflict in their homeland. Since the diaspora live in relatively wealthier societies, far away from the conflict theatre, and are not directly subject to the consequences of violence, they might pose as more 'national' or 'ethnic' than their counterparts who remain in their place of origin (Brinkerhoff 2011).

In most cases, multiple drivers are embedded in a conflict situation. It is thus important to understand as to which structural causes act as the primary trigger for conflict and which is the derivative. For example, while economic underdevelopment acts as the primary driver, unemployment becomes the derivative. If we address the former, the latter will be automatically taken care of. However, irrespective of the nature of drivers, all types of conflict and recurring violence deteriorate the security environment which in turn negatively affects economic development.

The concern for the integration of security and development policies emanates from the involvement of developed countries as aid donors to the conflict-ridden fragile States. The increasing realization that state fragility allows the emergence of ungoverned spaces, which act as incubators of terrorism and pose a serious threat to their own security in a borderless globalized world, has led the developed countries to take active initiative for conflict mitigation in poor countries (Hout 2009). However, donor countries are faced with the dilemma as to how development aids can be used for conflict prevention, conflict mitigation, and promoting the human security in the recipient countries. Although the direction of causality between these two policy goals is still hazy, and some tension exists between the notion of security-informed development and development-mediated security, a focus on supporting governance reforms acts as a potential link between security and development objectives (Youngs 2007). Democratic governance is viewed as fundamental for poverty reduction, conflict resolution, and promotion of human security. The fragility can best be addressed through governance reforms, establishment of rule of law, strengthening the anti-corruption measures and political inclusion, and building of institutions. As investments in the conflict-ridden poor countries are unable to unfold their impact due to the existence of political instability, it is realized that development policy can only achieve its effects if security measures are designed to restore the political stability in them (Faust and Messner 2004). This realization has led the donor countries to adopt a policy of securitization of development in fragile States. By way of designing security-linked conditionality for development aids and a number of instruments linking elements of governance and security, on the one hand, and adding more and more development-oriented components to the security policy design, on the other, donor countries are making effort to dovetail both the concerns for development and security in fragile States.

While state fragility is manifested in almost half of the world's sixty poor countries like Sudan, Congo, Palestine, Somalia, Colombia, Afghanistan, Rwanda, Burundi, Sierra Leone, Guinea Bissau, Haiti, Timor-Leste, Yemen, and so on, the concern for the international community, the fragility syndrome persisting in some regions of a country is a serious concern for its national government. Taking cue from the international experiences in conflict mitigation, the national governments can also devise a suitable response combining the security and development concerns to address their regional fragility and in turn can also contribute to the international discourse on state fragility. The present book deals with the regional fragility in India's NER.

Next to Jammu and Kashmir, NER comprising Arunachal Pradesh, Assam, Manipur, Meghalaya, Mizoram, Nagaland, and Tripura, euphorically called the seven sisters, has become the second soft underbelly of India. The state-centric security perception arising out of cold-war stratagem, Nehruvian model of integration of the hills of region through Assam, Nehruvian tribal development policy, aspirations of the Assamese to make Assam a nation-province for the ethnic Assamese, post-partition landlocked location, growth of proto-nationalism, failure of democratic conflict-resolution mechanism, failure of the states to provide effective security of life, high level of corruption, poor governance, practice of the politics of violence, large-scale immigration across the border, low economic growth, high incidence of unemployment—the interplay of this host of factors has created a material base fertile for thriving insurgency in the region.

The present study explains the dynamics, both external and internal, of unfolding of issues relating to the (in)security and (under) development in the NER. The state-centric and orthodox security perception during the early decades of independence kept India's land borders in general and northeastern borders in particular inaccessible so that they could act as the natural barriers against any external aggression. In fact, till the 1962, an Sino-Indian border conflict, development of the NER had become the hostage of traditional approach towards border security. During the 1960s, an intense feeling of territorial insecurity precluded any major investment in the NER as India was not sure whether it could hold the NER in case of any simultaneous thrust from China and Pakistan across the Chicken's Neck (Das 2002a). By the time Pakistani threat to India's northeastern border melted down following the liberation of East Pakistan and a policy of forward engagement put in place by way of reorganization of the NER in 1972, gain in external security environment was outpaced by deteriorating internal security environment with the rebellion of the Nagas, Mizos, and Meiteis getting into momentum. The fast proliferation of ethnic militancy since the 1980s has made it difficult for development to take root.

Thus, the dynamics of external security threats, underdevelopment, and deterioration of internal insecurity environment arising out of grievance-based ethnic militancy have led NER into a conflict trap. The book analyses such social and political dynamics and suggests context-specific measures for breaking the conflict trap in the NER.

It pleads for a three-pronged strategy for breaking the vicious cycle of insurgency and underdevelopment in the NER. First, integrating the economy of the NER to that of South Asia and Southeast Asian regions through active economic diplomacy which will then break the landlocked condition of the region, a sine qua non for initiation of market-led economic development, on the one hand, and which will, on the other hand, provide the necessary leverage to the Indian State to address the internal insecurity issues arising out of cross-border operation of the ethnic militant groups. Second, entails adopting a community-based development model which is more suitable for the conflict zones particularly where the institution of state has failed as an agency mainly due to ingression of anti-state and anti-people forces into the state structure. Use of community-based organizations as a development agency will not only improve state–society relationship, but also invigorate internal production, consumption, and distribution. Third, is improving the governance through the practice of politics of inclusion as counter to politics of identity and reining on corruption.

Chapter 1 focuses on the implications of India's external security concern in the eastern border for the development of the NER. That is, as to how the development prospect of the NER has been affected due to external security concern arising out of hostile relations between India and the neighbouring Pakistan and China. How India's conduct of foreign policy in relation to her neighbours delimited the external perimeter as well as inner contents of development of the NER. Chapter 2 focuses on the political dynamics emerging out of the efforts of the Indian State to integrate the tribal communities inhabiting the northeastern fringe and the efforts of the ethnic Assamese elite to convert Assam as the nation province of the Assamese. It makes an attempt to explain as to how the conflict between these two approaches—integration approach of the Indian state and making-Assam-a-nation-province-of-the-Assamese approach of the ethnic Assamese elite had ultimately led to the dismemberment of Assam, which might be viewed as India's response towards internal adjustment to counter external security threats. Chapter 3 focuses on the social, economic, and political dynamics behind the growth of fragility syndrome in the NER. Chapter 4 captures the interlinkages between in(security) and (under) development by way of accounting for economic costs of insurgency in the NER that has contributed to the onset of the conflict trap. Finally, Chapter 5 outlines the policy measures for breaking the conflict trap.

CHAPTER 1

Security, Engagement, and Development

Stability of a political system, its security, and economic development seem to be positively correlated. In an international system of States, a particular state can hardly attain these goals in isolation. International relations, economic diplomacy, regional as well as international forum are used by nations to enhance their 'national interest' and improve the 'security environment'. A good neighbourly relation, no doubt, improves the security environment, whereas a hostile relation not only deteriorates it but also negatively affects 'national development' by way of forcing the hostile neighbours to divert resources from development to defence needs. The arms race between China and India as well as India and Pakistan and escalating defence budget in these countries are cases in pointers. The tenuous relations between India and Pakistan as well as between India and China have impeded development in South Asia, as their political relations defy the interdependent logic of nature which knows no political boundaries. For example, India, China, and Bangladesh share the Brahmaputra river basin. Any intervention in this basin by the upstream countries will certainly have an impact upon the downstream nations. Similarly, the great Himalayan range is spread across India, China, Pakistan, Afghanistan, Nepal, Bhutan, and Myanmar which requires collective action for maintaining the Himalayan ecosystem. As States, in the international state-system, compete for global resources, friendly competition yields better results in achieving national interest than rivalries. In fact, rivalry between nations might lead to conflict, pose a threat to peace, and deteriorate the security environment. International investors generally shy away from fragile security environment of a state and its political instability.

India's security is linked directly with the neighbouring countries with which she has borders. India shares land borders with seven countries. The length of India's land border with the neighbouring countries is given in Table 1.1.

Table 1.1: India's Land Border with the Neighbouring Countries (in km)

India–Pakistan	3,244
India–China	4,056
India–Bangladesh	4,351
India–Myanmar	1,643
India–Nepal	1,751
India–Bhutan	700
India–Afghanistan	106
Total	15,851

Source: MOD (1999–2000).

Besides land border, India shares maritime boundaries with seven countries. India has two coastlines that are over 7,600 km long with island territories on both sides. India's Exclusive Economic Zone (EEZ), thus, extends to over 2,000,000 sq km. The island territories in the east are 1,300 km away from our mainland and are virtually adjacent to our Association of Southeast Asian Nations (ASEAN) neighbours (MOD 1999–2000). This geographical setting has, no doubt, tremendous security implications.

Any development in the neighbouring countries has serious implications for India. Besides immediate neighbourhood, India's 'extended neighbourhood', that is, broader security horizon—defined as regions with which economic, social, cultural, and environmental linkages result in overlapping security interest—includes countries of ASEAN, Central Asia, Gulf regions, and the Indian Ocean Community (MOD 1997–8).

Foreign policy of a country intends to promote its national interest, protect its sovereignty, territorial integrity, and security. Modern states view the conduct of foreign relations as a dynamic exercise which enables them to build national capability in order to respond optimally to new opportunities and challenges in a fast-changing world. While the art of conducting foreign relations has far-reaching implications for national development, it is no less important for the development and security of the bordering regions. Although it is of utmost interest to study as to how India's relations with her immediate neighbours affected her pace of development in last fifty years, we do not propose to undertake this ambitious task here. Our objective is far narrower.

We, rather, intend to focus on the implications of India's security concern in the eastern border for the development of the bordering NER. That is, as to how the development prospect of the NER has been affected due to security concern arising out of hostile relations between India and neighbouring Pakistan and China. How India's conduct of foreign policy in relation to her neighbours delimited the external perimeter of development for the NER. Being surrounded by Bangladesh, Bhutan, China, and Myanmar, it is only natural that unlike any other region, the NER will be directly affected by India's conduct of relations with these countries. A state-centric traditional security perception tends to consider the bordering regions as vulnerable to external threats. This perception, in turn, informs the other state-led development actions in the bordering areas. Thus, the conduct of India's foreign policy not only sets the outer perimeter of development for the NER, it also largely determines the inner content of development.

The development interest of the NER, as determined by its geostrategic location, lies in greater interaction with the markets across the international borders. The length of the land border between the NER and the neighbouring countries is shown in Table 1.2.

Table 1.2: Length of the Land Border between the Northeastern States and Neighbouring Countries (in km)

NER–Myanmar	1,643
NER–China	1,000
NER–Bhutan	650
NER–Bangladesh	1,880
Total	5,173

Sources: Das and Purkayastha (2000); IIE (2001); MOD (1999–2000).
Note: Lengths are not precise.

It may be noted that about 33 per cent of the country's total international land border falls in the NER, involving four out of seven countries sharing their border with India. As the NER shares 98 per cent of her border with the neighbouring countries and merely 2 per cent with mainland India, cross-border exchange forms an important parameter in her development strategy. Moreover, the NER shares substantial common resources with areas across the border. And the historically developed pattern of production and communications is also oriented towards markets across the border. As a result the utilization of natural resources of the NER calls for greater cross-country subregional development cooperation.

It is our utmost interest to examine the role of the Indian state in promoting this development interest of the NER through her conduct of external relations since independence. It has already been pointed out that the implications of India's relations with neighbouring China, East Pakistan, and Myanmar for the NER are far deeper than any other regions of the country. As the region is surrounded by these countries, and inhabited by the social groups having affinities with their counterparts across the borders, and being isolated from the 'mainland of India', having traditional markets across the border, non-cooperation from the neighbouring countries would put the region in a suffocating situation without any hope for it to grow and develop. Thus, the interest of the region and its long-term security lie in strong and mutually beneficial relationship between India and her eastern neighbours. Although, the same also holds good for national interest, for the NER it is a precondition for her survival. It is from this point of view that we shall look at India's conduct of foreign policy in relation to her neighbours.

As the conduct of foreign relations is a dynamic process and keeps on changing in commensurate with the global change, it may be of some conceptual value to divide the temporal space of India's relations with her neighbours into three broad phases. Phase I starts from independence and extends up to 1962, the year in which Sino-Indian border conflict took place. This border conflict not only brought a change in India's foreign policy, but also a significant policy-shift towards the NER having far-reaching effects on its future evolution. Phase II covers the entire time span starting from 1963 to the end of the Cold War in 1991, the year in which erstwhile Union of Soviet Socialist Republics (USSR) had collapsed. This phase is characterized by two Indo-Pak wars of 1965 and 1971. The emergence of Bangladesh as an independent country in 1971 has significant bearing on the security and development of the NER. Phase III covers the period since 1992 characterized by onset of globalization paradigm where India is increasingly seeking forward engagement with her neighbours.

Phase I (1947–62): From Asian Solidarity to Hostility

The concept of 'Asiatic-Federation' and the notion of 'Asianism' as mooted by the Indian National Congress even prior to independence (Bandopadhyaya 1991) as part of its anti-colonial struggle and later articulated and operationalized by Jawaharlal Nehru, the first prime minister of India, was fully compatible with security and development concern of India in general and the NER in particular. The idea emphasized the need for close cooperation among the postcolonial Asian societies, having common experience of colonial exploitation and suffering, for their future progress. But this project 'Asianism' was destined to crumble with the sharpening of competitive and overlapping interests between India and Pakistan, and China in the South Asian region. India, interspersed between West and East Pakistan, has always been perceived as the principal threat to the territorial integrity and national security of Pakistan. In fact, partition of the country on the basis of religion, and formation of Pakistan without any territorial contiguity has instilled in it an in-built threat perception of India. However, in 1948, the two neighbours took arms against each other over the Kashmir issue, fell apart, and became archrivals, which rendered the first blow to the 'Asian Solidarity' movement.

Nehru tried to advance this movement by befriending China and sidelining Pakistan. The Treaty of 1954 between India and China, and the Bandung Conference of Afro-Asian countries held in 1955, in which Nehru and Chou En-Lai played the leading roles, seemed to have restored the credibility of the movement to some extent. But the overlapping interest of both India and China in the Himalayas and their competitive claims for regional power brought Sino-India honeymoon to an abrupt end. The Chinese occupation of Tibet in

1950 made India alert of her northern security. It also panicked the Himalayan kingdoms of Nepal, Bhutan, and Sikkim. These Himalayan states had been a part of British India's defence system as the buffer states between India vis-à-vis China and Russia. In relation to these kingdoms, British India adopted a forward policy whereby they enjoyed internal autonomy, but their external relations were directed by British interest (Lamb 1960). Independent India adopted the same policy for Bhutan and Sikkim. The Treaty of Peace and Friendship signed between India and Bhutan in 1949 and Indo-Sikkim Treaty of 1950 were a mere continuation of the British legacy. In order to restrict Chinese advance beyond Tibet, both India and Nepal entered into a Treaty in 1950. As part of her Forward Policy in the Himalayas, India, throughout the 1950s, pushed its administration to catch up the McMohan Line in the north. Like India, China also had security interest in the Himalayan kingdoms. In fact, China viewed Tibet to be her palm and Nepal, Bhutan, Sikkim, Ladakh, and North-East Frontier Agency (NEFA), presently known as Arunachal Pradesh, as its five fingers (Thapliyal 1999). This conflicting interest in the Himalayas appeared to have led to the Sino-Indian border conflict in 1962. India was taken aback by the sudden Chinese attack, and, in absence of any defence preparedness, had to swallow a humiliating defeat. The story is well known and we do not intend to repeat it here. What is important for us is the significance of the 1962 border conflict for India in general and the NER in particular.

First, there had been divergence of views among the Indian policy makers on the possible security threat to our northern and northeastern borders. Sardar Patel, the first union home minister warned Nehru against the security threat arising out of Chinese annexation of Tibet and urged to review our border policy and security and favoured speedy development of communication/transportation infrastructure (Verghese 1996). But Nehru's idealist assessment of Sino-Indian relations and his conviction to settle scores with China through dialogue led him to underestimate the threat perception. This underestimated security perception coupled with Nehru's policy towards tribal development, and perhaps the traditional views that inaccessible borders act as deterrent to external aggressor, had a significant bearing on the slow pace of development in the NER during Nehru's regime (1947–64).

Second, the 1962 border conflict put the last nail in the coffin of the Asian Solidarity movement. Asianism as an element of India's foreign policy had built in promises for the landlocked and isolated NER. With the unfolding of future, the NER could have been more focused to the market networks of neighbouring countries, which would have helped in breaking her isolation. The potential the region derives from her geostrategic location to act as the gateway not only to Southeast Asia, but also to Central Asia remained unexplored.

Third, Government of India's (GoI) handling of the 1962 crisis and its failure to protect the lives and properties of people had generated tremendous psychological shocks in the minds of the people of the region. India's role in protecting the interest of the region was viewed as inadequate. This deeper feeling of being dumped at the moment of crisis helped anti-India forces within and strengthened their position in disengaging people against the Indian state.

Fourth, India's defeat in 1962 had largely tarnished her image in South Asia and her small neighbours started drifting towards China in their bid either to assert against Indian influence or to gain more by siding with the more powerful rival. This had made it difficult for India to immediately advance her interest through the improvement of bilateral relations after the collapse of Asiatic perspective.

Fifth, in order to fill the 'population vacuum' near Sino-Indian border in Arunachal Pradesh, a massive resettlement program was launched after 1962. A sizeable section of East Pakistani Chakma refugees were rehabilitated in Khagam, Miao, M'pen, Kharsang, and Chowkham areas of northeastern Arunachal Pradesh in subsequent years (Das 1995). This has created the breeding ground of the present Chakma-Arunachalee ethnic conflict.

Last, India's defeat in 1962 encouraged Pakistan to seek a military solution to Kashmir problem. After the Nehru–Liaqat Ali pact of 1950,[1] Pakistan had improved its security position significantly by signing Mutual Defence Assistance Agreement in 1954 with the United States and joining the South East Asia Treaty Organization or SEATO[2] (1954) and the Central Treaty Organization or CENTO[3] (1955). With the establishment of USA–Pakistan–China axis following the

1962 Sino-Indian border conflict, Pakistan's attempt to forcibly occupy Kashmir had led to Indo-Pak war of 1965.[4] The implications of this war for the security and development of the NER were obvious. With growing Indo-Pak animosity, not only the NER's traditional market in East Pakistan remained inaccessible, the political space therein had also been freely used to destabilize the region. Both the Naga and Mizo rebellions that started during 1950s and 1960s, respectively, were sheltered and nourished by Pakistan through its eastern wing (Bhaumik 1996; Roychoudhury 1986). The internal insecurity of the region grew tremendously with China's backing the Naga and Manipuri insurgents (Hazarika 1995; Horam 1988; Tarapot 1996). Sandwiched between China and East Pakistan, not only had the external security threat to the NER increased manifold, its internal insecurity also became a prime concern. This fast-deteriorating security environment had a negative bearing on the development prospect of the region.

Phase II (1963–91): Replication of Cold War in South Asia

Beset in a cold-war paradigm and besieged by Pakistan–China–USA axis, India had limited diplomatic options to address her security threats. India took a pro-USSR position to thwart any future threat to her security arising out of her rivals and adopted an 'inward looking' strategy for national development. It may be noted as a digression that the mixed-economy model characterized by public-sector dominance in basic industries and infrastructure and private participation in consumer goods and services reveals the state's concern for speedy national development. The realization that 'without development there can be no security' loomed large in the minds of the policy makers. What is important to us is to note that the use of scarce resources was strictly guided by the criteria of its maximum spread effects and inter-sector growth impulses. The fact that any major investment in the NER, due to her geographical location, would result into less spread effects compared to other regions in the mainland, did not support any large-scale public sector investment in the region. As a result, state-sponsored development had largely bypassed the region. We shall have occasion to deal with this issue in more detail later.

Be that as it may, the outbreak of liberation movement[5] in East Pakistan (1971) provided India to break her 'cordoned-off' security environment. Throwing the garb of 'non-alignment' India entered into a treaty[6] with the USSR (1971), used bipolar world contradiction in her favour, intervened in favour of liberation movement in East Pakistan, and played a decisive role in bringing Bangladesh as an independent nation. This event had far-reaching implications for India's security concern in general and security and development of the NER in particular.

First, India relieved of permanently from Pakistani threat to her security on the eastern border. A friendly Bangladesh would also expect to improve internal security conditions in the NER by debarring insurgents to use Bangladesh territory against India.[7]

Second, a scope has emerged to re-establish the NER's traditional markets and communication networks which had been snapped due to partition. As Bangladesh needed corridors through Indian land to ease out movement of goods and people from one part to another interspersed by Indian territory, India's landlocked northeast also needed corridor through Bangladesh. There exist mutually beneficial grounds for cooperation in this regard.

Third, Bangladesh economy after long years of colonial exploitation, and then twenty-four years of internal colonial exploitation by Pakistan, subsequently, ravaged by the liberation war, was in a bad shape. It was only natural for Bangladesh to look up to India for necessary financial and technological help creating a space for Indian industries and trade in Bangladesh economy. Since the resource structure between Bangladesh and the NER is of complementary in nature, it was expected that the NER's resource-oriented products would find a vent in Bangladesh leading to a close cooperation particularly between eastern region of Bangladesh and the NER.

Fourth, there arose a hope that the issue of immigration and influx from erstwhile East Pakistan into ethno-sensitive northeast would be amicably resolved. The northeastern societies would get away with the burden of war refugees.

Fifth, the victory against Pakistan in 1971 would improve India's image in South Asia, which she had lost in 1962, to a large extent, and would enable her to advance the national interest in the neighbouring countries through bilateral channels.

Last, with improved external security environment on the northeastern border, India would be in a better position to address the internal insecurity dimension in the NER arising out of ethnic insurgencies, inter-ethnic schisms, and underdevelopment.

With the emergence of Bangladesh, India's threat perception in her northeastern border, her national interest in Bangladesh in terms of trade in general, and the NER's trading interest in particular had improved to some extent. But this Indo-Bangladesh honeymoon was short-lived. Bangladesh followed a pro-Indian foreign policy during 1971–5, followed by the anti-India position during 1976–88, and then a strategy of cooperation since 1989. As the image of dominating India was always permeating the consciousness of Bangladesh, the shifts and swings in Indo-Bangladesh relations might well be explained as Bangladesh's efforts to come out of the Indian influence. Bangladesh's perception of her security threat from India increased significantly following the incorporation of Sikkim into Indian Union in 1975. The interfering attitude of the Indian state in internal matters of her small neighbours, the socio-political compulsions at home arising out of Hindu–Muslim relations in South Asia, and the cold-war paradigm that had been replicated in South Asia following Indo-Chinese conflict in 1962 and Indo-Pak war in 1965—all had a strong bearing behind the drift of Bangladesh towards China–USA axis in post-Mujib era.

So far the interest of the NER is concerned, opening up of overland trade, although in a very limited way, gave some respite. Mineral products and forest products from Meghalaya, Mizoram, and Tripura found ready markets in Bangladesh (RIS 1998–9), which otherwise would have not been cost-effective. However, the potential of border trade between the NER and Bangladesh largely remained untapped primarily because of inadequate engagement of both the governments in this regard. As Bangladesh was facing escalating deficit trade balance with India,[8] and seeking its redress through higher imports, she (Bangladesh), as a result was not much encouraged to utilize the border trade potential in full which would only further complicate her balance of payment situation. As 'border trade' is a strategic parameter having a great significance for the development of northeastern economy, Indian government could have accommodated it in a far better way by adjusting its overall bilateral trade interest with Bangladesh. Either the growth-generating significance of border trade was underrated, or the economic diplomacy in this case was not informed by geopolitical wisdom of the Indian state.

However, the issue of the NER's access to her traditional communication channels through Bangladesh, for example, Tripura's access to Calcutta via Bangladesh territory, has only partially materialized only in case of passenger movement.[9] Moreover, the threat of infiltration across the border loomed large throughout with growing political uncertainty in Bangladesh characterized by frequent flood, poverty, over-population, and utter underdevelopment. Besides this identity threat to indigenous societies, real or perceived, the use of insurgent groups by Bangladesh for bargaining other wider issues with India, particularly during strain bilateral relations, remained as a built-in threat to the internal insecurity of the NER.

While India's relations with Bangladesh has a direct bearing on the security and development interest of the northeastern states of Assam, Meghalaya, Mizoram, and Tripura, the Indo-Myanmar relations have similar implications for Manipur, Nagaland, Mizoram, and also partly for Arunachal Pradesh.

India's security interest in Myanmar is evident from her geostrategic location. Myanmar shares an equally significant border with both India and China. The northern frontiers of Myanmar constitute a tri-junction with Bangladesh, China, and the eastern frontiers of India. Myanmar is also an important country lying on the rim of the Bay of Bengal. The south-eastern coast of Myanmar is close to the Nicobar and Andaman Islands. Moreover, Myanmar is also the corridor through which India can reach out to 'extended neighbourhood' regions of Southeast Asia. Hence, presence of any hostile power in Myanmar is viewed inimical to Indian interest. As far as the interest of the NER is concerned, people living in the states of Manipur, Nagaland, Mizoram, and Arunachal Pradesh, besides having ethno-cultural affinities with the people across the border, had developed traditional trading relations. Their access to markets across the border is far easier than the markets even in Assam plains. As a result, sharing of resources and communication channels including traditional trade routes across the border is an essential precondition for their future development. Moreover, because of commonality in ethnic origin and historically developed cultural ties between the people across the NER–Myanmar border, the possibility of spilling over of social discontents across the international boundary has made the internal security of the NER vulnerable.[10]

Thus India's Myanmar policy has direct bearing on the security and development of the NER. India's Myanmar policy is largely informed by her threat perception from China. The threat of communism from China brought India and Myanmar closer to each other during the 1950s and the 1960s. In order to accommodate the interest of Myanmar, Nehru had even gone to the extent of giving up the Indian claim on Kabaw Valley, with which sentiments of people of Manipur were strongly associated. The bilateral relations were institutionalized by the 1951 Treaty of Peace and Friendship. Several treaties followed thereafter in order to strengthen mutual economic, technical, and cultural ties. But with the realization of Myanmar that instead of pro-Indian position its security interest will be better served in adopting a neutral policy between India and China, and with the signing of Treaty with China in 1960, Indo-Myanmar relations started losing its warmth. During 1962 Indo-China conflict, Myanmar took a neutral position and subsequently tilted towards China.

In post-1962 period, until the breakdown of the cold-war paradigm, India's Myanmar policy was largely informed by her antagonistic relations with China. While China was increasingly engaging herself in constructive cooperation with Myanmar in terms of building roads and other infrastructure, and thereby strengthening her economic and security interest in Myanmar, India maintained studied silence. Increasing supply of Chinese arms and ammunitions into Myanmar, alleged access of Chinese naval force in Myanmar ports, Chinese assistance to Naga and Manipuri insurgents, and use of Myanmar territory by the insurgents as bases for conducting subversive activities against India added to India's anxiety without any adequate response. Thus, India's disengagement in Myanmar and its failure to evolve any counter-strategy not only harmed the Indian business interest in Myanmar, but also alarmingly escalated the internal insecurity in the NER and blocked its prospect of development. However, the situation started improving from early1990s to which we shall come back later.

Although the Asian Solidarity Movement died a premature death in 1962, the geoeconomic compulsions for such regional cooperation became stronger with the unfolding of time leading to the launching of the South Asian Association for Regional Cooperation (SAARC) in 1985 with Bangladesh, Bhutan, India, the Maldives, Nepal, Pakistan, and Sri Lanka as its members. Pregnant with tremendous scopes for the development of the South Asian region, SAARC has a special promise for enhancing development interest of the NER.

First, the programme of trade liberalization among SAARC members brightens up the possibility of utilization of full potential of 'border trade' between NER and Bangladesh.

Second, with the growth of cooperation among the member countries, it might have been possible to link up Indian communication system, that is, roadways, railways, and waterways, to that of Bangladesh which could have broken the geographic isolation of the northeast to a large extent providing the necessary vent for the products of the NER in Bangladesh markets.

Third, the idea of subregional development and the concept of growth zones mooted in the SAARC Expert Group report have tremendous implications for the development of the NER. The Expert Group has identified three subregions, northeastern sub-region, consisting of parts of Nepal, Bhutan, India, and Bangladesh, the southern region consisting of a part of India, the Maldives, and Sri Lanka, and the northwestern region consisting of India and Pakistan, for initiating subregional development programmers (RIS 1998–9). The NER is covered in SAARC's first growth zone area, that is, the northeastern subregion. Since the basic idea of development cooperation at the subregional level is to put development in the subregion on a faster track, SAARC's zonal-growth approach has the potential to address the development interest of the NER.

Fourth, once the subregional cooperation takes off in SAARC's northeastern subregion, it is possible to gradually supplement the mainland of India as the principal source of manufactured exports to the NER through various joint ventures particularly between the NER, Bangladesh, and Bhutan. This will lead to the increasing utilization of the NER's natural resources on the one hand, and equally enable

Bangladesh and Bhutan to improve their trade balance vis-à-vis India (Thapa 1999).

Fifth, the proposal for the creation of an Asian Energy Grid mooted at the Trilateral Business Summit in Dhaka in 1998 by the prime ministers of Bangladesh, India, and Pakistan has a great relevance for the development of the NER. In spite of having the highest potential for generating hydroelectric power in the country, which has been estimated at 31,857 MW out of 84,044 MW available for the country as a whole, that is, 38 per cent of total, only about one per cent had so far been utilized (CEA 1997). With Asian Energy Grid in operation, demand would not pose any further barrier in utilizing this huge untapped power potential. The revolutionizing role of power in economic development of the region hardly needs any clarification.

However, the promise embedded in SAARC for the NER does not appear to turn into reality in foreseeable future. Bilateral relations among the member countries, time and again, overshadowed the collective interest of the group. SAARC deliberations were disrupted in 1985 and 1990 because of tensions between India and Sri Lanka on the Tamil ethnic problem, again during disputes between Nepal and Bhutan on the question of the Nepalese whose citizenship rights in Bhutan were questioned by the Bhutanese government, following the destruction of the Babri mosque in 1992 and the resultant agitations in Bangladesh and Pakistan against India, and now the military coup in Pakistan in 1999 that led to India's reluctance to participate in SAARC meetings in which the military regime of Pakistan is also a member (Dixit 2001).

The most worthwhile achievement of SAARC in the realm of economic cooperation has been the creation of Preferential Trading Arrangement (SAPTA) among its members and its subsequent transition to South Asian Free Trade Area (SAFTA).[11] If the gain from trade liberalization is any indicator, this regional grouping has generated much frustration than hopes. The share of intra-SAARC trade in world trade of SAARC countries has increased from 2.4 per cent in 1985 (Mel 2007) to only 4.8 per cent in 2008 while the share of intra group trade in ASEAN accounts at 25.8 per cent, for North American Free Trade Agreement (NAFTA) at 40 per cent in 2008 (Jain and Singh 2008). Achievements are, no doubt, abysmal. Needless to say that unless the two big powers, India and Pakistan, who play the dominant role in SAARC affairs, shrug off their myopic state-centric positions in favour of regional cooperation, it is hard for SAARC to take off. This realization, perhaps, has led the member countries to look beyond SAARC for partnership in their development strides. India's engagement in other alternative regional development forums and her adoption of the Look East Policy, which will be taken up next, become more meaningful while viewed from this perspective.

Phase III (1992 Onwards): Globalization and the Era of Forward Engagement

With the collapse of the Soviet Union in 1991, the cold-war paradigm came to an end. Bipolar world became unipolar with the United States of America at the helm of global affairs. The launching of the globalization programme by the US and its allies has completely changed the spectrum of cold-war strategic partnerships. The international system, greatly relieved of bipolar tensions, has generated a tremendous scope for the states to forge new partnership in order to strengthen their security environment and enhance national interest. Responding to these new challenges, the Indian state has formulated, and is still formulating, new approaches in conduct of her foreign policy. Some of these new policy shifts, particularly in relation to neighbouring countries and regions having direct bearing on the security and development of the NER, are of our particular concern.

India's China Policy started changing from isolation to engagement following the visit of the then Prime Minister Rajiv Gandhi to China in 1988 and reciprocal visit by Chinese Premier Li Peng in 1991, after a gap of 31 years of such state visits. The successive visits by the President and the Prime Minister of India to China in 1992 and 1993, respectively, and the reciprocal visit by Chinese President in 1996 had considerably released the tensions in Sino-Indian relations. The Agreement on the Maintenance of Peace and Tranquility along the Line of Actual Control (LAC) in the India-China border areas, signed on 7 September 1993, during the visit of India's prime minister to China, has laid down the framework for maintenance of peace and tranquillity along the LAC between India and China. Under the agreement, the two sides agreed to resolve the boundary question through peaceful and friendly consultations. Both the countries committed not to use force against other by any means. Pending an ultimate boundary settlement, both agreed to 'strictly respect and observe' the LAC between the two sides and not to overstep it by any activity. Where there are differences on the alignment of the LAC, the experts from both countries would 'jointly check and determine' (MOD 1993–4) where the LAC lies. Both the countries agreed to undertake a series of Confidence Building Measures (CBMs), including the reduction of military forces deployed along the Indo-China border in conformity with the principle of 'mutual and equal security' (MOD 1993–4). Besides this, the 'Agreement on Confidence Building Measures in the Military Field along the LAC in the India-China Border Areas', signed in November 1996 during the visit of Chinese President Jiang Zemin to India, inter alia, stipulates that neither side shall use its military capability against the other side, and includes provisions for negotiating the reduction of limitation of forces from mutually agreed geographical zones along the LAC, the prior notification of military exercises, and service to service contacts (MOD 1996–7).

These two agreements followed by the visit of the India's President Mr K.R. Narayanan to China in 2000 and the visit of the Chinese leader Mr Li Peng to India in January, 2001, have significantly scaled down the elements of mistrust in Sino-Indian relations that has aggravated further following the Pokhran II explosion in May, 1998. Notwithstanding Chinese involvement in Pakistan's nuclear weapon and missile programs that remains as a major concern for India, the role of China in Indo-Pak war on Kargil in 1999 seems to be an indicator of shifts in China's India policy as well.

Be that as it may, the compulsions arising out of the forces of globalization, challenges faced by the nations in evolving a new global order, and forging new strategic partnership seem to have largely informed the remaking of foreign policy of both India and China towards each other since 1990s. Although no durable structure of cooperation between them has yet evolved, China's realization of the fact that the 'common ground' between India and China 'far outweighs' the differences between them, and the need 'to elevate Sino-Indian relations to a new height in the 21st century' for 'peace and development in Asia and the world at large' seem to enhance the possibility of establishing a 'constructive partnership of cooperation' between these two Asian neighbours in foreseeable future (Li Peng 2001). Successive visits by Chinese Premiere Zhu Rongji in 2002, Wen Jiabao in 2005, President Hu Jintao in 2006, and Premier Wen Jiabao in 2010 to India and counter-visits by Indian leaders like Prime Minister A.B. Vajpayee in 2003, Prime Minister Manmohan Singh in 2008, and President Pratibha Devisingh Patil in 2010 to China have considerably eased out Sino-Indian relations and initiated the process for the growth of structured multi-level engagements between these two countries in areas like trade and commerce, counterterrorism, security, defence, water resources, judiciary, cultural, education, science and technology, audit, personnel, finance, investment, and labour.

The economic cooperation between India and China in the field of trade and commerce has improved significantly. The volume of trade between them has increased from US$ 49.22 million in 1990–1 to US$ 37,950.67 million in 2007–8 signifying a whopping increase of about 771 times in 18 years[12] and then to US$ 42,441.90 million during 2009–10.[13] Besides the growth bilateral trade, opening up of Nathula Pass[14] on 6 July 2006, after 44 years, for cross-border trade has been a remarkable event in Sino-Indian relations.

Besides trade, volume of mutual investment is also on the rise. The cumulated value of Contractual Chinese Investment (Projects) in India till October 2008 is US$ 22 billion. The cumulative realized value till October 2008 of the contractual Chinese investment in projects is US$ 7.7 billion. Similarly, the cumulative Foreign Direct Investment (FDI) from India into China in the projects till October 2008 is US$ 816 million in 406 projects.[15]

Following the visit of Indian defence minister to China in 2006 and signing of a Memorandum of Understanding (MoU) for exchanges and cooperation in the field of defence, there have been growing bilateral contacts between the defence personnel primarily through annual defence dialogue and joint training exercises.

In spite of significant improvement in bilateral trade and exchanges in other areas, the overall Sino-Indian relation is yet to shrug off the Cold War hangover. The mutual distrust still looms large between these two Asian neighbours. While the Indian state is not comfortable with growing Chinese influence on countries bordering India and a significant section of the Indian political elite perceive that China extends active support to Pakistan's proxy war against India, the Chinese political elite feel that India is playing in the hands of the western powers to contain China. The growing Indo-USA strategic partnership particularly in the fields of nuclear energy and defence cooperation is viewed to be inimical to Chinese interest. In fact the security and development of NER has been, to some extent, caught in the crossfire of Sino-Indian rivalries for regional power and supremacy.

Like India's China policy, Indo-Myanmar relations also started improving since the early 1990s. Removal of idealistic elements and injection of more sense of pragmatism in formulating India's policy towards Myanmar have led Indian policy makers to realize that India's support to pro-democracy movement led by Aung San Suu Kyi against the military regime would in no way enhance India's security and national interest in Myanmar. As there was no sign of relinquishing power to the National League for Democracy, led by Suu Kyi, which emerged victorious following 1990 election, by the Myanmar military regime, India had little choice other than to come to terms with the existing regime. Informed by China's intensive engagement in Myanmar, growing insecurity in the NER arising out of various insurgent activities, and the strategic importance of Myanmar in India's Look East Policy, India had adopted a more pragmatic Myanmar policy setting aside its interest in democracy in Myanmar, one of the major irritants that strained Indo-Myanmar relations for so long.

The visit of the vice foreign minister of Myanmar, Mr U. Baswe, to India in 1992 helped both the countries to clear their misconception about each other. Both entered into agreements for the development of areas along the international border and for working together against the forces of destabilization, militancy, and insurgency. A border-trade agreement was signed in 1994 allowing trade to flow through selected customs posts along Moreh (Manipur)–Tamu (Myanmar) and Champhai (Mizoram)–Hri (Myanmar) sectors. Although only the Moreh–Tamu sector has been officially opened for trade pending the infrastructural development in the other sectors, the Agreement, no doubt, has profound importance for the NER (for details see, Das and Purkayastha 2000). As part of India's further engagement in Myanmar, Indian government has already constructed the Tamu–Kalemayo road in 2001. This road is expected to be a part of the ambitions Asian Highway Project conceived to link up Singapore with New Delhi via Kuala Lumpur, Ho Chi Minh City, Phnom Penh, Bangkok, Vientiane, Chiang Mai, Yangson, Mandalay, Tamu, Dhaka, and Calcutta (Dhar 2000). Once the Asian highway becomes a reality, it will remove the communication bottleneck of the landlocked states of Manipur, Mizoram, and Nagaland to a large extent and will pave the way for their integration with the Southeast Asian region. Besides economic opportunities, improved Indo-Myanmar relations also have direct bearing on the security environment of the NER. Increasing cooperation between the security forces of India and Myanmar in dealing with cross-border insurgent activities has compelled many of the northeast insurgent groups to shift their bases from Myanmar. The visit by General Maung Aye, vice president of the Myanmar government to India, in November 2000, has opened up the scope for India's multifaceted and comprehensive engagement in Myanmar which will enable India to address her concerns about security and development in the NER in a far better way.

Visits by the Indian president in 2006, the external affairs minister in 2007, the vice president in 2009, and the external affairs minister in 2010 to Myanmar, and the counter visits by Myanmar's chief of general staff and the home minister in 2006, the deputy minister, foreign affairs in 2007, the vice senior general and the vice chairman of State Peace and Development Council (SPDC) in 2008, the foreign minister in 2008 and the chairman of SPDC in 2010 to India have facilitated multi-level bilateral engagements in areas like roads, hydroelectricity, hydrocarbon, multi-modal transport, telecommunications, medical, information technology, oceanographic surveys, security, and defence.

The volume of Indo-Myanmar trade has also registered a substantial rise. From US$ 55.2 million in 1991–2, the bilateral trade volume has gone up to US$ 995.35 million in 2007–8, indicating an eighteen-fold increase. The Indo-Myanmar trade volume has gone up to US$ 1,497.77 million during 2009–10.[16] India stands as Myanmar's fourth-largest trading partner after Thailand, China, and Singapore and also Myanmar's second largest export market after Thailand, absorbing 25 per cent of its total exports.

Myanmar and India have agreed to work for the multi-modal project in Sittwe port in Myanmar's western Rakhine coast with Indian investment of US$ 100 million. Implementation of the Sittwe port project mainly aimed at promoting trade with ASEAN. India's interest in the Kaladan project stems from latter's potential to transform the economy of its northeastern states. Once completed—it is expected to take about four years—the Kaladan project will facilitate the transport of goods by road and river from the landlocked northeastern states and the Kaladan river would run from Mizoram in India through Myanmar's Chin, the Arakan states, emptying into the Bay of Bengal, to Sittwe port, and from there on to markets in Southeast Asia.

India's investment in Myanmar had reached US$ 35.08 million in three projects as of January 2006, out of Myanmar's total foreign investment of 7.985 billion dollar since late 1988. India's latest and main involvement in Myanmar includes the building of the US$ 133 million Reed-Falam road, optic fibre link project between India's Moreh and Myanmar's Mandalay, and natural gas exploration and production at block A-1 and A-3 in Myanmar's Rakhine offshore areas being carried out under a consortium led by South Korea's Daewoo International Corporation, in which the ONGC Videsh Ltd of India holds 20 per cent of stake and the Gas Authority of India Ltd (GAIL), 10 per cent. India has been seeking to buy gas produced from the two Myanmar blocks and ways of laying the pipelines from Myanmar to India are also being sought.[17]

India has also established an Indo-Myanmar Centre for Enhancement of IT Skills (IMCEITS) at Yangon with Indian assistance of two million dollars. This Centre, run by Indian professionals, is equipped to train 1,000 youth every year initially who will be awarded a diploma of the Pune-based Centre for the Development of Advanced Computing (C-DAC) which is an institution under the Ministry of Information Technology. India has set up a heavy turbo-truck assembly plant in Myanmar with the help of TATA Motors in 2010. Besides these, an India–Myanmar Industrial Training Centre, Myanmar-India Centre for English Language Training (MICELT), and Myanmar-India Entrepreneurship Development Centre (MIEDC) were also established.

However, India's engagement in Myanmar compared to that of China is still insignificant. If the NER is to leapfrog from the abyss of economic underdevelopment by way of integrating her economy to that of the neighbouring countries, Indo-Myanmar relations have to strike deeper routes and cross-border synergies need to be harnessed for the benefit of both the countries.

Indo-Bangladesh relations also started improving since early 1990s. The normalization of bilateral relations was largely facilitated by 'Gujral Doctrine' and return of democracy in Bangladesh. India's forward engagement started with the visit of External Affairs Minister Mr I.K. Gujral to Bangladesh in 1990. Within a short span of time a number of irritants like the issue of providing Tin Bigha Corridor to Bangladesh, sharing of the Ganga water, and repatriation of the Chakma refugees to Bangladesh, were effectively resolved. India provided the Tin Bigha Corridor to Bangladesh in 1992. The accord on sharing of Ganga water was signed in 1997. And the problem of Chakma refugees was solved with their repatriation from camps in Tripura to Bangladesh in 1998. This repatriation of Chakma refugees has, no doubt, a great significance for ethno-sensitive psyche of the people of the northeast. This achievement in India's Bangladesh policy would appear to have reduced inter-ethnic schism arising particularly out of Mizo-Chakma conflict in Mizoram and Arunachalee–Chakma conflict in Arunachal Pradesh in more than one way by scaling down the threat of further Chakma ingression in Mizo and Arunachalee territories, respectively.

In spite of a number of bilateral irritants like operation of Indian insurgent groups from Bangladesh, influx of illegal Bangladeshi migrants into the northeastern states of India, disputed enclaves, fencing of Indo-Bangladesh border by India, provision of transit corridor by Bangladesh to India, addressing the problem of secular Bangladeshi balance of trade deficit vis-à-vis India, facilitating access for Bangladeshi products into Indian markets, skirmishes between the border security forces of the two countries, the bilateral relations, particularly in case of trade and commerce, has grown steadily. The volume of trade has gone up from US$ 117.87 million in 1980 to US$ 3,175.34 million in 2007–8.[18] The bilateral trade stands at US$ 2,688.44 million during 2009–10.[19] Besides merchandise trade, both the governments are in the process of creating healthy investment climate for mutual private sector collaboration and investment. In November 2007, the GoI had removed the prohibition on investment into India by citizens of Bangladesh or entities incorporated in Bangladesh, allowing investments that have prior approval of the foreign investment policy board of the GoI. A total of 185 FDI and joint venture investment proposals from India worth over US$ 438 million have been registered with the Board of Investment, Government of Bangladesh in sectors such as agro industry, textiles, chemicals, and engineering industries till September 2008. A number of trade facilitation measures have been initiated to promote cross-border trade and connectivity between the two countries.

Flow of trade across the NER–Bangladesh border has also registered significant increase. From Rs 154 crores of cross-border trade during 1998–9, it has increased to Rs 688 crores during 2009–10 (Barbhuiya 2011). However, the transit facilities through Bangladesh, being a major interest of landlocked NER, have not yet been materialized. If the economy of the NER is to develop, there are hardly any cost-effective options other than the transit through Bangladesh. Whatever improvement in bilateral relations has taken place, the interest of the NER has not yet been addressed. Of course, with the deepening of bilateral relations in recent years, a silver lining has appeared in the horizon as Bangladesh has agreed on principle to provide transit facilities between the NER and mainland India. The sooner it materializes, the better it is for the NER.

Look East Policy

The Look East Policy has been adopted by India as a response to change in the global politico-strategic order following the collapse of erstwhile USSR, end of bipolarity, and launching of the globalization programme. It is, indeed, a step towards throwing India's 'South Asia' centric image and reorienting her foreign policy from cold-war bipolarity to globalized multipolarity in the sphere of trade and commerce. Since the adoption of this policy in 1992, in spite of initial hiccups, Indian ruling elites could market it aggressively. Within a decade and half, India succeeded to engage the ASEAN and other East Asian countries in comprehensive bilateral as well as multilateral frameworks. The complementarities of objective economic, political, and strategic reality that exist between India and ASEAN have acted as the driving force behind the fast-growing partnership within a remarkably short span of time.

The substantial increase in the volume of two-way trade between India and ASEAN, between India and China; the comprehensive engagement including defence cooperation with some of the ASEAN members like Malaysia, Indonesia, Vietnam, and Thailand; the free-trade agreement with ASEAN; and upgradation of India–ASEAN relationship to summit-level partner are some of the indications of the success of the Look East Policy.

The Look East strategy has dramatically lifted the Indian foreign policy framework out of the box, which was fixated for long on Pakistan. Neither India carries any negative 'historical baggage' in relation to the Southeast Asian countries, nor is there the 'Pakistan Factor' to be countered. This policy exhibits a metamorphosis of India's foreign policy from idealism to pragmatism. Unlike Nehruvian global outlook, this is less rhetoric and more strategic. Following the upward turn in national growth and emergence of critical areas of strength like information technology, biotechnology, pharmaceutical technology, space and remote sensing technology, nuclear technology, and defence technology, India is not seeking friendship only on the strength of her political support, but has created complementarities for sustainable and mutually beneficial engagements. This policy is, thus, pregnant with opportunities for the nation and the region as well. However, how far the dream will translate into reality depends on how quickly the northeastern states can create the synergies for trade and developmental cooperation across the border.

The 'Look East Policy' is, indeed, the first ever policy adopted by India to engage with Southeast Asia in general and ASEAN in particular. In fact, India had no policy in place to enter into structured interaction with ASEAN beforehand (Kaul 2001). Although ASEAN was formed in 1967 and made considerable progress during the 1970s and the 1980s, India, being a Soviet ally during the later stage of the cold war, initially viewed it as a USA surrogate and an extension of American security alliance in Southeast Asia. The Cold-War exigencies compelled India to adopt (in the 1980s) an inconsistent view of pursuing an opposite political goal (by supporting the Soviet–

Vietnam-backed Heng Samrin's government in Kampuchea) and seeking economic cooperation from the ASEAN member countries (Kaul 2001). India preferred not to engage with ASEAN, but wanted to strengthen her relationship with the members of ASEAN through bilateral engagement.

However, with the adoption of the Look East Policy in the early 1990s, the India–ASEAN relationship immediately took root. India was made a Sectoral Dialogue Partner in 1992 and upgraded to the status of a Full Dialogue Partner in 1995. She was admitted as a member in the ASEAN Regional Forum (ARF) in 1996. India became a summit-level partner in 2002 (Nanda 2003). However, India's desire to be a member in ASEAN+3, where China, Japan, and South Korea interact with the ASEAN on economic and regional security issues, has not yet been materialized reportedly due to the opposition from China.

Although the Look East Policy focuses on India's engagement with ASEAN, the policy also looks beyond and envisages intensifying India's engagement with the East Asian countries particularly China, South Korea, and Japan. As a broader outlook, this policy is a manifestation of India's interest to engage herself with all types of institutional mechanisms that promote economic development, peace, regional stability, and cooperative security in all the Asian countries. India is interested to join in the Asia Pacific Economic Cooperation (APEC) formed in 1989 where twenty-two countries along the Pacific Rim interact. India is also interested to be a part of the Asia–Europe Meeting (ASEM) initiated in 1996 where twenty-five EU member states, the European Commission, ten ASEAN members, China, Japan, and South Korea participate.

As India is not a member of APEC, the Look East Policy focuses mainly at two levels, namely, engaging the ASEAN and the East Asian countries in order to promote mutual benefits.

India is forging relationship with ASEAN countries both through bilateral as well as multilateral engagements. Multilateral institutional mechanisms like ARF, India–ASEAN Summit, and India–ASEAN Business Summit provide the platform through which India interacts with ASEAN. India's engagement with ASEAN has two major dimensions, namely, economic and security cooperation.

India has signed a Comprehensive Economic Cooperation Agreement (CECA) with ASEAN on 8 October 2003, during the second India–ASEAN Summit at Bali. The CECA has institutionalized the India–ASEAN relationship. It proposes for the establishment of an India–ASEAN Regional Trade and Investment Area (RTIA) as a long-term objective. The CECA seeks to deepen economic linkage between India and ASEAN, lower costs, increase intra-regional trade and investment, increase economic efficiency, establish a Free Trade Area (FTA) in goods, services, and investment through progressive elimination of tariff and non-tariff barriers, liberalization of trade in services, and establishment of competitive regime for the promotion of investment.

Both India and ASEAN, as per the CECA, intend to cooperate in three sectors of their economies. Right from agriculture, fishery, forestry, mining of oil and gas, power generation and supply, cooperation is sought in the manufacturing of automotive, drugs and pharmaceuticals, textile, petrochemicals, garments, food processing, leather goods, light engineering goods, gems and jewellery processing, handicrafts, small and medium enterprise development. In areas of science, technology, and service, cooperation will be extended in media and entertainment, health, education, tourism, construction, Business Process Outsourcing (BPO), e-commerce, Intellectual Property Right (IPR), and biotechnology. Cooperation is also proposed in areas of transport and communication.

The CECA, under Article 7, provides for Early Harvest Programme (EHP) in order to accelerate its implementation. Under EHP, a number of commodities are enlisted on which early reduction of tariff has been proposed. This agreement entered into force on 1 July 2004 and by 2011 it was supposed to be fully implemented.

A similar CECA between India and Singapore was signed on 29 June 2005, which had become operational from 1 August 2005. A Framework Agreement for establishing free trade between India and Thailand was also signed on 9 October 2003 in Bangkok, Thailand. The Framework Agreement covers FTA in goods, services and investment and other areas of economic cooperation. The Framework Agreement also provided for an Early Harvest Scheme (EHS) under which eighty-two common items of export interest to both the sides have been agreed for elimination of tariff on a fast-track basis.

India and Malaysia have agreed to enter into similar kind of agreement. A Joint Study Group (JSG) has already been constituted for drafting the agreement framework between India and Malaysia in 2005. Both the countries have adopted the Joint Study Group Report on 11 August 2007 which has paved the way for an India–Malaysia (CECA) signed in 2010.

India and Indonesia have also signed an MOU in 2005 for setting a JSG for the preparation of CECA between them. The first meeting of India–Indonesia JSG to study the feasibility of setting up a Comprehensive Economic Cooperation Agreement with Indonesia was held in Jakarta in 2007 (MEA 2007–8). The CECA document is ready for launching.

The ASEAN–India Trade Negotiating Committee (TNC) was constituted and several meetings have been held so far. The ASEAN–India TNC is undertaking negotiations to establish an ASEAN–India RTIA which includes an FTA in goods, services, and investment. Due to difference of opinion on Rules of Origin, the EHP, agreed under the Framework Agreement, on goods could not be implemented. The new time frame for FTA in goods has been agreed. The ASEAN–India FTA (AI–FTA) has been signed in 2009. Agreement has been reached on the Rules of Origin. The TNC is now negotiating the negative or sensitive list, the modality for tariff reduction and elimination, dispute settlement mechanism, etc.

In case of India–Thailand CECA, tariff concessions on eighty-two items of EHS list began in 2004. The tariffs on these items have been brought to a zero by both sides in 2006. India–Thailand TNC has been constituted and discussions are being held on the text of FTA, Rules of Origin, Dispute Settlement Mechanism, and Sensitive List. As per the Framework Agreement, the FTA in goods would commence from March 2005. However, due to difference of opinion on certain issues, this deadline could not be met. Negotiations for FTA in services and investment have also begun. Bilateral trade increased from US$ 2,286.89 million during 2005–6 to US$ 3,189.96 million during 2006–7 to US$ 4,671.68 million during 2009–10.[20]

In spite of the slow progress in implementing the CECAs, two-way trade between India and ASEAN has registered a perceptible rise. In fact, a clear trend is emerging in the direction of India's foreign trade in recent years which exhibits a gradual shift from the dependence on the economies of the West and increasing reliance on the economies of Northeast and Southeast Asia. India's economic interaction in terms of her export destination and source of import in post globalization era is intense in five regions of the world, namely, the European Union (EU), North America, ASEAN, West Asia and North Africa (WANA), and Northeast Asia. The trend since mid-1990s suggests that Indian business has woken up to the new realities that have emerged in Asia and accordingly adjusting to them by reorienting their exports and imports.

Both India's export to and import from ASEAN have registered almost four-fold rise in 2004–5 over 1996–7. During 2010–11, the volume of India–ASEAN trade accounted for US$ 50.1 billion. ASEAN-4, namely, Indonesia, Malaysia, Singapore, and Thailand have strong trade linkages with India. India's export to and import from these countries has registered considerable rise since the beginning of this century. India's trade with Myanmar, Philippines, and Vietnam is also rising since 1990s. Brunei, Cambodia, and Laos, the three weak ASEAN members, are also gradually experiencing rising trend in their trade relations with India.

Beyond ASEAN, the Look East Policy also focuses on the restructuring of her relationship with the North East Asian countries particularly China, South Korea, and Japan.

India and South Korea have agreed in 2004 to establish a JSG to prepare a road map for a Comprehensive Economic Partnership Agreement (CEPA) between the two countries. Although the group has already submitted its report suggesting measures for further deepening of economic relations in terms of trade in goods and services, facilitation of investment and cooperation in the field of science and technology, charting out the synergies of both the economies, the CEPA has not yet signed. However, India–South Korea bilateral trade, investment, and economic cooperation has experienced a spurt since the India–ASEAN CECA in 2002. India's export to South Korea has registered a rise of 340 per cent in 2005–6 (April–December) over

1996–7. South Korea absorbed about 2 per cent of India's total export in this year. India's import from South Korea has registered a rise of 544 per cent during the same period. About 3 per cent of India's total import came from South Korea in 2005–6 (April–December). Two-way trade between these two countries has registered a growth of about 468 per cent in 2005–6 (April–December) over 1996–7. The volume of trade has reached US$ 11,997.12 million during 2009–10.

India's trade with Japan has not shown much sign of improvement. India's export to Japan has registered a marginal rise of 54 per cent in 2005–6. Indo-Japan relation provides a plausible explanation for this low-intensity trade and economic cooperation between these two countries. Japan has been the most trusted ally of USA all through the cold-war era and even in post-Cold War regime Japan plays the role of the hub in Asia Pacific region in USA's 'hub and spike' regional policy. The cold-war calculus, thus, prevented any significant bilateral relationship to grow between India and Japan. Moreover, as Japan's foreign policy is exclusively focused on the Asia Pacific, although India is, no doubt, an Asian power, but it is Pacific rather than 'Asia' that counts most for Japan (Jain 2002). Although Japan, as the main initiator, excluded India from APEC, the Indo-Japan relation has taken a turn towards the better, following the improvement in Indo-US relation since the beginning of this century. With economic growth picking up and as India established herself as the hub of global IT, Japan does not want to miss the investment opportunity arising in India and hence the two countries have stepped up measures to engage with each other. Japan seeks to embrace India as a 'global Partner' (Jain 2002) and has increased Official Development Assistance (ODA) for infrastructure development, investment in joint ventures and wants to create more close private sector partnerships. India and Japan have agreed to form a JSG in 2005 in order to focus on measures required for a comprehensive expansion of trade in goods and services, investment flows, and other areas of economic relations between the two countries. India–Japan JSG has already been set up and Department of Economic Affairs is the nodal point on the Indian side. The two sides have also initiated negotiations for a CEPA in early 2007 and signed the same in February 2011.

Japan presently ranks sixth largest in cumulative FDI flows into India. Japanese companies have made actual investment of US$ 4.63

billion between April 2000 and November 2010. Most direct Japanese investment in India is in manufacturing industries, focused on the domestic market.

Since 2004, India has been the largest recipient of Japanese ODA. Till March, 2011, the total cumulative commitments of Japanese ODA to India reached Yen 3,320.3 billion. Disbursement of ODA totalling to Yen 123.8 billion during 2010–11 has been the largest amongst all countries accounting to 18.3 per cent of Japan's all ODA disbursement. This ODA continues to play an increasing role in areas including infrastructure development, environment, energy, poverty reduction, and social-sector development (MEA 2007–8).

It has, thus, been evident that India's Look East Policy has produced a significant result in terms of forging trade and economic cooperation with ASEAN as well as North East Asian countries. In fact, Indian foreign policy mandarins are so much enthused with the success of this policy that they are working towards the replication of this model in relation with the West Asian countries and have adopted a similar 'Look West' policy.

Let us now turn our attention to the question as to what will be the implications of this Look East Policy for the growth and development of the NER which is India's gateway to the Southeast Asia.

Needless to mention, the NER is one of the most underdeveloped regions of India. Being completely landlocked, positioned at the periphery of national geography, history, and culture, far away from the national market centres and surrounded by neighbouring countries of Bhutan, Bangladesh, China, and Myanmar, development interest of this region will be better served if she is positioned in a broader canvas of East and Southeast Asia rather than remaining completely blindfolded towards them. In fact, the development of this region has become the hostage of India's state-centric security perception towards her eastern borders for long. Of course, the deteriorating security environment in India's eastern borders during the cold-war rivalries was not unfounded as the anti-Indian forces (read Pakistan and China) made concerted efforts to chop the NER by prodding and sponsoring ethnic insurgent movements across the border.

However, the post-cold war foreign policy calculus of India in general and the Look East Policy in particular has created an enabling environment which can break the landlocked condition of the NER by way of opening to the markets of the neighbouring countries across the border, establishing joint-venture enterprises and bringing cross-border investments for the development of infrastructure, manufacturing, and services. The cross-country initiatives for economic cooperation like Bay of Bengal Initiative for Multi-Sectoral Technical and Economic Cooperation (BIMSTEC) and Mekong-Ganga Initiative (MGI) which have been launched to add more substance to India's Look East Policy and where India plays a significant role can be instrumental to remove some of NER's developmental predicaments.

There is a proposal to construct a 1,360 km Trilateral Highway from Moreh (India) to Mae Sot (Thailand) through Bagan (Myanmar). The detailed project report on this is under progress (Strategic Digest 2004). With the signing of the India–Thailand FTA in 2003, there has been a steady rise in two-way trade with Myanmar and spectacular growth in Sino-Indian trade, and the prospect of the NER becoming a hub of transit trade is only brightening.

However, except these possibilities, the Look East thrust has not yet produced any perceptible tangible benefit for the NER. The opening of border trade with Myanmar, as per the provision of Indo-Myanmar Border Trade Agreement (1994), could hardly make any impact on the regional economy (Das 2000). India's ASEAN trade flows through the sea route. The continental route that passes through NER–Myanmar–Thailand has not yet been considered safe and cost effective. As a result, coastal states are being benefited out of India's growing relation with ASEAN. The continental land bridge, that is, NER will come in focus once Sino-Indian economic cooperation takes root and focuses on the realizing the potential of cross-border trade between southwest China and northeast India (Das 2005b), utilizing the synergies across the border between India and Myanmar (Das and Thomas 2005) and establishment of a strong resource-industry linkage in the region (Das 2005c) which will enable the regional economy to offer something in exchange of her imports from the neighbouring countries and make the cross-country trade sustainable.

What is to be noted at this juncture is that the Look East Policy has made it possible to factor into the development interest of the NER in India's foreign policy making. Active engagement of the governments, business, and other agents of change in the practice of India's Look East Policy coupled with the planned and prudent use of Non-lapsable Pool for enhancing a strong resource-industry linkage may only enable the NER to translate her geopolitical disadvantage into geoeconomic advantage.

Although the derivatives of this policy like the formation of the MGI and BIMSTEC bear tremendous potential, till now this eastern thrust could not create an enabling environment conducive for fuelling the growth in the NER. In fact, the complementarity on which the India–ASEAN relation is thriving is absent in the region. No doubt, by leveraging the Look East Policy, India will be in a better position to manage the affairs in her northeast, but before northeast positions herself in this Look East framework she has to do her homework right and achieve something which she can offer to her neighbours. For becoming the front-line states in India's Look East Policy, northeastern states have to set their house in order and transform the region as a hub of growth and peace. Otherwise instead of continental India, that is, the NER, maritime India, that is, the coastal states, will be the super highway for two-way communication between India and East Asia. Although there does not exist any trade-off between the continental route and maritime route to East Asia, rather they compliment each other in reinforcing the bond, nonetheless once a structure develops there is a tendency for it to continue. It is easier to be a pathfinder than establish oneself as the better option through competition and contestation. For this to happen the ruling elite in the region need to sit across the table and prioritize the regional goals, identify the areas of comparative advantages and use the 'North East Initiative' programme to create the enabling environment conducive for regional growth.

Thus, the competition among ASEAN, India, China, South Korea, and Japan within and beyond the framework of ASEAN and cooperation among them for synergies is certain to open up the opportunities for trade through continental routes in future and dilute the negative 'border effects' on trade, investment, and economic development.

Bay of Bengal Initiative for Multi-sectoral Technical and Economic Cooperation

What is important from the NER's point of view is India's growing engagement in different subregional level development initiative involving the neighbouring Asian and Southeast Asian countries. The launching of the BIMSTEC in 1997, involving Bangladesh, India, Myanmar, Sri Lanka, and Thailand and subsequently joined by Myanmar, Nepal, and Bhutan, has a profound development and security implications for the NER. BIMSTEC is the first grouping of its kind in which two ASEAN members have come together with five countries from South Asia to form an association for economic cooperation. The forum aims at utilizing the untapped resource potential in the subregion for mutual benefits. It has already identified thirteen priority areas such as transport and communications, energy, trade and investment, tourism, technology, fisheries, agriculture, cultural cooperation, environment and disaster management, public health, people-to-people contact, poverty alleviation, and counter terrorism and transnational crime for cooperation, with each country assuming a specific responsibility for coordination. Important projects which are currently under consideration by the forum include the Asian Highway Link which has already been mentioned earlier, Asian Railway Network and a Natural Gas Pipeline Grid (MEA 1998–9). All these projects have tremendous implications in removing the communication isolation as well as utilizing the untapped resources of the NER. While the NER will have access to Asian Highway through the Imphal–Tamu feeder road, as indicated earlier, the railway system of India and Myanmar will be linked at Dibrugarh railhead. This will enable the NER to have access to Asian Railway Network.

However, BIMSTEC subregional cooperation is only in its infancy. Even after a decade of its existence, no perceptible progress has been made except a few feasibility studies particularly undertaken by Asian Development Bank having subregional developmental implications.

Bangladesh, Bhutan, India, and Nepal Growth Quadrangle

Besides BIMSTEC, another cross-country subregional initiative having wider ramifications for the NER is the Growth Quadrangle involving Bangladesh, Bhutan, India, and Nepal Growth Quadrangle (BBIN-GQ) under the SAARC initiative. Although this initiative is still in embryonic form, working modalities for cooperation have already been finalized in the second meeting of foreign secretaries of the four countries in Kathmandu held on 17 July 1998. The BBIN-GQ is to follow a project-led approach to cooperation in the core economic sectors of multimodal transportation and communication, energy, trade and investment, tourism, utilization of natural resources, and environment. These projects will be supportive of and complementary to national plans of the countries in the Growth Quadrangle. The projects will make best use of neighbourhood synergies and the resources and expertise within the subregion will be given priority in their implementation. A prioritized, practical, action-oriented, time-bound and incremental approach will be followed in selection, development, and implementation of projects having immediate impact as well as large infrastructure projects with long gestation (MEA 1998–9).

Nepal, besides looking after the overall subregional cooperation efforts, will also coordinate projects in the areas of tourism and multimodal transportation and communication. Bangladesh will coordinate the projects involving energy and utilization of natural resources. Bhutan and India will coordinate projects involving environment and, trade and investment promotion, respectively (MEA 1998–9). Once the BBIN-GQ takes off, it will provide yet another space where development interest of the NER can be accommodated.

In a study organized by Asian Development Bank, it has been suggested that among the BBIN countries there exists enormous trade and investment potential. The study also suggested measures like BBIN-FTA, BBIN investment area, BBIN integrated sectors, BBIN HRD resource bank, BBIN banking enclave, BBIN information hub and statistical system, and a BBIN secretariat. These measures would go a long way in creating linkages not only with the rest of the region, but also in targeting the world market (Pankaj 2004).

However, although the project BBIN-GQ is pregnant with promises for the development of NER, no perceptible progress is yet in sight. It has largely remained at conceptual stage and hence could hardly make any difference to the ground realities as far as NER is concerned.

The Meckong–Ganga Initiative

Another cross-country subregional cooperation programme having long-term implications for the development interest of NER is the MGI. The Initiative traces its origin to 'Mekong Basin Project' involving Myanmar, Cambodia, China, Laos, Thailand, and Vietnam. Later, this project has been widened to accommodate India. The Inaugural Ministerial Meeting on MGI took place in Vientiane at the initiative of India and five Southeast Asian countries in November, 2000. The Vientiane Declaration upholds the common desire of the member countries to develop relations and better understanding among themselves for enhancing friendship, solidarity, and cooperation. Tourism has been identified as an immediate priority area having significant potential for development in the subregion (Baruah 2001). For tourism development, studies are to be conducted into joint marketing, facilitating travel in the region and expanding multi-modal communication and transportation links. Although this initiative is still under process, its future unfolding will have significant impact on the NER which is India's gateway to Mekong Basin region.

It has already been pointed out that bilateral trade and economic cooperation between India and countries in Southeast Asia are growing fast following India's adoption of the Look East Policy. Except, some limited cross-border trade particularly aiming at easing out the life of the bordering people across Indo-Myanmar border, the trade between India and countries in Southeast Asia flows through sea routes benefiting coastal regions as the land route through continental NER is considered to be unsafe and also due to the non-existence of bilateral as well as multilateral agreements on transport and other trade facilitation measures like certification, standards, and so on. Thus, the NER has not yet much benefited out of the MGI.

Kunming Initiative

Besides these institutionalized cross-country subregional development initiatives, opinion across the countries is getting crystallized for the formation of another growth quadrangle involving China, India, Myanmar, and Bangladesh, which has found an expression in the 'Kunming Initiative' articulated in an international conference at Kunming, the capital of Yunnan Province of China, in August 1999. The basic objective of this initiative is to promote cross-country subregional development cooperation among contiguous regions of eastern/NER of India, south-west China, northern Myanmar, and

Bangladesh. However, this initiative still remains at the Track II domain and is yet to be institutionalized.

***

Thus, the opportunities arising out of post-cold war global scenario and India's positive response to them have created a favourable external condition for the development of the NER through cross-country development initiatives. The geostrategic location of the region necessitates an integrated cross-country subregional cooperation for development. This can only be achieved by placing NER in a larger South Asian as well as Southeast Asian canvas. For so long this perspective was not in the consciousness of the Indian state. As a result, India's conduct of foreign policy towards her neighbours was not much informed of the development interest of the NER prior to the 1990s. Moreover, the underestimation of external security threat to northeastern border prior to 1962 and overestimation of the same at least during 1962–71 appear to have negatively influenced the central public-sector investment decisions in this region. The development interest of the NER has, thus, become a hostage to state-centric mindset. The failure of economic diplomacy of the Indian state, even after 1971, to address the development predicaments of the NER through forward engagement with Bangladesh and Myanmar had further added more life to the disabilities of the region. Even the SAARC framework, which could have been utilized to remove some of the predicaments of the NER, has largely remained imperative primarily due to Indo-Pakistan rivalry. The external perimeter of development as defined by India's relations with the neighbouring countries is, thus, not in harmony with the geostrategic location of the NER. The resultant underdevelopment partially caused by this disharmony has got entangled with other ethnic aspirations leading to the creation of an environment of internal insecurity in the region. This has made it extremely difficult for private initiatives to reap the benefits from the opportunities unbundled following India's renewed engagement with the neighbours and Southeast Asian neighbourhood.

Having outlined the impact of India's foreign policy on the development interest of the NER, an attempt will be made in Chapter 2 to understand the policy of the Indian state towards integration and development of the NER in an adverse external security environment.

Notes

1. The pact, signed on 8 April 1950, ensures security to the minorities residing in India and Pakistan. It also provides equality to the minorities in both the countries.
2. The SEATO was launched in February 1955, based on the Manila Pact signed on 8 September 1954. It had been modelled after the NATO in order to provide anti-communist shield to Southeast Asia. It was dissolved on 30 June 1977.
3. Modelled after the NATO, the CENTO was formed in 1955 in order to contain the erstwhile USSR by having a line of strong states along the USSR's southwestern frontier. It was dissolved in 1979.
4. India's humiliating defeat in 1962 Sino-Indian border conflict encouraged Pakistan to launch an attack against India in 1965. Pakistan underestimated the strength of the Indian Army and miscalculated that once Pakistani Army enters Kashmir, Kashmiris will revolt against India which will make their job easy.
5. The liberation movement started following the denial by the west Pakistani political elites to allow Awami League (AL), East Pakistan based political party, to form the government under the leadership of Sheik Mujibur Rahman in spite of the fact that the AL won the majority of the seats (167 out of 300) in the National Assembly in 1970 election. This had intensified the feeling of deprivation in East Pakistan against its Western counterparts and ultimately led to outbreak of the liberation movement.
6. The Indo-Soviet Treaty of Peace, Friendship and Cooperation, signed on 9 August 1971, provided a security shield to India against external threats as both the countries resolved to mitigate such threats collectively.
7. This expectation has not been materialized as Indo-Bangladesh relations had run into rough weather following the assassination of Sheik Mujibur Rahman in 1975 and with the growth of mutual suspicion between India and Bangladesh during the Zia-ur-Rahman regime which has led Bangladesh to tilt towards China.
8. The negative balance of trade for Bangladesh vis-à-vis India has increased from US$ 93.17 million in 1980–81 to US$ 2,661.10 million in 2007–8, almost a twenty-nine-fold rise (Das 2008a; Export–Import databank [see note 13]).
9. It took about 30 years for India and Bangladesh to start passenger transport service across the border between the NER and Bangladesh. On 19 September 2003, Agartala–Dhaka bus service was introduced. Bangladesh is still reluctant to provide transport corridor between the NER and mainland India. For the details on the political economy of non-cooperation on the part of Bangladesh see Das 2008a.

10. A significant Chin population from Myanmar migrated to Mizoram at different points of time of disturbances in their homeland. This immigration has hostiled the host Mizo community and subsequently led to Mizo-Chin conflict in Mizoram. For details, see http://eng.chro.org/index.php?option=com_content&task=view&id=126 & Itemid=26.
11. The SAFTA came into being on 1 January 2006. It aims to eliminate trade barriers among the SAARC countries by phases. Contracting countries are supposed to reduce tariff to 20 per cent by 2007 and bring down further to zero by 2012 by way of eliminating tariff, non-tariff and para-tariff barriers.
12. Data found in CD format provided by CMIE electronic databank (www.cmie.com).
13. See http://commerce.nic.in/eidb/iecnt.asp (accessed on 21 July 2011).
14. Nathu La, located at a height of 14,400 feet, connects Indian state of Sikkim and Tibet Autonomous Region (TAR) of China. It was a traditional trans-Himalayan trade route which was closed following the Sino-Indian border conflict in 1962. On the Indian side, a trade mart has been set up at Sherathang, a few kilometres below the Nathu La. On the Chinese side, the trade mart is located at Rinchangang in TAR. The political significance of the agreement to open up this route is far more important than economic benefit that will accrue to the people across the border in these two countries. This agreement is an indirect recognition of the fact that Sikkim is a part of India and Tibet is a part of China. This mutual indirect recognition of each other's territorial claims appears to have resolved the long standing Sino-Indian disputes in this sector.
15. See meaindia.nic.in/meaxpsite/foreignrelation/china.pdf (accessed on 16 November 2011).
16. See http://commerce.nic.in/eidb/iecnt.asp (accessed on 21 July 2011).
17. See http://english.peopledaily.com.cn/200612/21/eng20061221_334729.html (accessed on 17 August 2008).
18. Data found in CD format provided by CMIE electronic databank (www.cmie.com).
19. See http://commerce.nic.in/eidb/iecnt.asp (accessed on 21 July 2011).
20. Ibid. See also (MEA 2007–8).

CHAPTER 2

Integration, Social Dynamics, and Strategic Vulnerability

Having discussed as to how the external security concern of the Indian state towards her northeastern border delineated the outer perimeter of development of the NER, it may be worthwhile now to delve into the other side of the story. That is, as to how this external security concern has impacted the process of integration of the NER with the national mainstream as well as its course of development.

Policy for Integration of NER

Unlike other regions, a distinct policy towards the integration of the NER is needed for the following counts.

First, both the civilizational and historico-political process of making of the Indian nation had bypassed the hills of the NER and, for all practical purpose, Assam was viewed as the 'last outpost' of Indian nationalism in the east.

Second, the tribal communities residing in the hills are of Mongoloid stock having racial links with their counterparts across the northeastern borders.

Third, the insular traditional tribal social structures had been governed by strict rules of exclusions.

Fourth, the incorporation of tribal authority structure into the British isolationist administrative set-up, that had created a political space for the coexistence of tribal and colonial interests, needed to be accommodated in postcolonial Indian federal structure.

Fifth, the existence of numerous tribes and their variegated stages of evolution along the tribe-nation continuum and the process of fusion and fission had made the task of their integration very delicate and sensitive.

It may be noted that the question of integration of the tribal entities has always been a Herculean task to all nations. Many 'civilized nations' of today had resorted to most cruel methods of subjugation/ assimilation or extinction in order to resolve this problem as part of their programme of nation-building. This unresolved question of tribal identity has undermined the viability of many a nations in the Third World countries. The colonial 'policy of isolation' of the tribal communities from the 'British Indian Empire', another extreme approach, had virtually bypassed the resolution of the problem which no modern state can adopt without a risk to its territorial integrity. India's response to this problem has been unique. An accommodative, autonomous, and federal approach has been evolved to resolve this unfinished agenda through integration in contradistinction with assimilation and isolation.

Policy of Integration through Assam

With the end of the 'British Paramountcy' on 15 August 1947, like hundreds of princely states in British India, the political status of Manipur and Tripura, the two protectorate princely states of the NER, as well as excluded and partially excluded hill areas lying along north and south banks of the Brahmaputra remained undecided. As the territorial space of British India following partition was divided between secular independent India and Islamic Pakistan, there was hardly any alternative left to the princely states and people of excluded or partially excluded areas of the NER other than to accede to or join in either of the two newly born states. The polarized political space arising out of territorial ambitions of both India and Pakistan had largely influenced the response of the hill communities as well as the two protectorate princely states in favour of joining in India. The process of incorporation of these areas started with the process of transfer of power. Following the Standstill Agreement (1947), the Federation of Khasi states joined in India. The Jaintia Hills, Garo Hills, Lushai Hills, North Cachar Hills were added to the territory of Assam. The princely states of Tripura and Manipur acceded to the Indian Union in 1948 and 1949, respectively. The Arunachal Hills were brought under direct administration within a remarkable short span of time. The Nagas, who were nurturing with the idea of independent Naga country and hesitant to join in the Indian Union, once and for all, were also persuaded to come to an agreement, that is, Hydari Agreement (1947) resulting into the inclusion of Naga Hills as a district of the state of Assam.

Thus, within a span of about two years of independence, the Indian state succeeded to incorporate the hitherto 'excluded'/'partially excluded'/'unadministered areas' as well as the princely states of the NER. Except Tripura and Manipur, where the centralized system of governance had already been in existence, other areas were added to Assam in view of her historico-geographical proximity to the hills and the people thereof. In fact, Assam and the Assamese society being the representative of national 'mainstream' in the region and having territorial contiguity and historically developed ties with the hill tribes, the integration of the hitherto isolated hill societies was sought through them (Das 1997).

The administrative policy towards these excluded/partially excluded/ unadministered areas was largely formulated on the basis of Report of the North East Frontier (Assam) Tribal and Excluded Areas Sub-Committee headed by G.N. Bordoloi, popularly known as the Bordoloi Committee. The Committee felt that the 'hill people have not yet been assimilated with the people of the plains of Assam' and 'the future of these hills now does not seem to lie in absorption', 'rather evolution should come as far as possible from the tribe itself but it is equally clear that contact with outside influences is necessary though not in a compelling way' (GoI 1948). The Committee noted the anxiety of the hill people about their land and their fear of exploitation from the plainsmen and advocated for sufficient measures to protect the tribal rights in land and forest and also for tribal customs and traditions (for further details, see Das 1995).

Following the recommendations of Bordoloi Committee tribal aspirations were subsequently accommodated in the Sixth Schedule of the Constitution through the creation of autonomous district/regional councils. The concept of Autonomous District Council (ADC) within the administrative framework of a state has been a unique federal response to the unresolved issue of tribal identity. These ADCs were given constitutional rights to look after the tribal interest in relation to land, forest, and culture. It may be noted that except Assam, the provisions of the Sixth Schedule were not extended to any other state having tribal population. It is perhaps because of the fact that the legacy of colonial isolation of the tribal communities was unique only in the NER. Although the creation of ADCs had, no doubt, undermined the authority of the province state, they have been viewed as necessary politico-administrative devices for furtherance of integration of the hitherto isolated communities with the national mainstream.

In tune with the Sixth Schedule, the Indian state, under the premiership of Jawaharlal Nehru, had evolved a broad policy framework concerning the administration and integration of tribal communities in India in general and that of the northeast in particular. The works of G.N. Bordoloi, the first chief minister of Assam; Sir Akbar Hydari and Jairamdas Daulatram, both of whom were governors of Assam; N.K. Rustomji (1973, 1983) and K.L. Mehta (NEFA Administration 1956), the two advisers to the governor of Assam; and Verrier Elwin (1958) had contributed to the formulation of a definite tribal policy which found its finer articulation in Nehru and subsequently came to be known as Nehru's tribal policy (Elwin 1958; Nehru 1989). His 'five fundamental principles' (Elwin 1958) for tribal administration and development were an attempt to strike a middle path between assimilation and isolation. Nehru's policy envisaged that the tribal 'people should develop along the lines of their own genius'. It favoured to preserve 'tribal rights in land and forests', and tribal 'social and cultural institutions'. It advocated against 'multiplicity of (development) schemes' in tribal areas and 'introducing too many outsiders into tribal territory'. The formulation of this tribal policy was largely informed of two principal concerns. First, the security concern of the tribal identities against possible run-over by the huge non-tribal Indian population as has been voiced by different tribal communities time and again from the days of Simon Commission (NNC 1993). Second, the security concern of the northeastern border was inhabited by people who remained out of the reach of Indian nationalism. Tribal identity preservation in the NER had, thus, been considered as an element of India's territorial integrity and its security. The provision of Sixth Schedule, only for the tribal communities in undivided Assam, and Nehru's tribal policy, which was largely followed for the tribals in NER in general and NEFA in particular, were not extended to other states having significant tribal population. This indicates that Nehru's tribal policy was, inter alia, also a part of geostrategic thinking.

All along the Nehru era, India largely viewed her northeast through this 'identity-security prism'. The major challenge as perceived by the Indian state was to integrate the hill areas without disrupting the traditional tribal socio-economic structures. The policy of least governance, least intervention, and relative isolation had a built-in element of least development. Nehru was well aware of the fallout of partition on the economy of the NER in terms of the region's loss of traditional transportation and communication linkages and markets across the border (Nehru 1989). He was also aware of the effects of recurring floods in Assam plains on its economic progress. He knew the economic content of cross-culture conflicts in the region (Nehru 1989). While the region needed large-scale public-sector investment for the reorientation of its transportation, communication, and market linkage for river-valley projects in order to save the agriculture sector from the onslaught of recurring flood, and for resource-based industries to harness the natural bounties for the welfare of local people, Nehru's tribal policy stood in the way. In fact, Nehru's tribal policy or his model of tribal integration was not compatible with large-scale economic development through structural change. As a result, the Indian state had adopted a welfare-oriented development approach towards the NER. This approach emphasized more on the development of human resource by investing in education, health, and other social services in order to generate 'feel-good' effects in the minds of the people.

A corresponding policy for structural change and resource-based growth was missing as this was not possible without disrupting the traditional tribal–social institutions. The economic development of Assam had, thus, become a hostage to Nehru's tribal policy. As the development of Assam is a precondition for the development of Tripura and Manipur, lying along the southern and eastern fringe of Assam, for geoeconomic reasons, they were also left in the backyard.

Be that as it may, the model of integration of the tribal communities through Assam had two other important implications. First, it added to heterogeneity of her population composition and thereby further weakened the claim of the Assamese elite to make Assam a 'nation-province', to use Baruah's (1999) term. It has also further complicated the cleavage structure in Assam's polity. This integration model not only added further force to the strong linguistic and religious cleavages that developed during the colonial regime, it also added new dimensions in the form of racial and religious cleavages as the tribal communities in the Naga, Garo, Khasi, and Mizo hills are of Mongoloid origin and are predominantly Christians. The politico-administrative structure evolved in Assam on the basis of the Sixth Schedule had created a political space more suitable for the practice of 'consociational' rather than 'majoritarian' politics. The non-realization of this political reality by the elite in Assam had later created unmanageable discontent among various groups to which we shall come back shortly.

Second, the post-partition population gains in Assam were, to some extent, compensated by the territorial gains in terms of the hill areas. The extension of administration and social services in the hills had created a space for the gainful absorption of the educated middle class. This had, to some extent, reduced the strain arising out of inter-ethnic competition for state privileges in the plains of Assam.

However, this model of integration faced two diametrically opposite challenges—one arising out of the Nagas' refusal to integrate themselves with India and the other from Assam's attempt to establish linguistic homogeneity in order to elevate her status to a nation-province. While Assam's initiative indirectly strengthened the Naga movement, the latter further reinforced the negative impacts of the former. The cumulative fallout of these two on the security environment has ultimately led to the abandonment of India's policy of indirect integration of the tribal communities through Assam in favour of direct integration through federalist solution. Let us first take up the issue of Naga integration.

Crisis of Integration through Assam Model in Naga Hills: Integration and Security Dimension

Naga movement for 'independence' has several dimensions. Here we do not intend to enumerate the long account of the six-decade old conflict in Nagaland. Our purpose is two fold—to focus on the security implications of the Naga insurgency and to examine the resultant response of the Indian state towards integration of the Naga Hills. This section is partly based on author's earlier analysis of Naga insurgency (Das 1997).

Right from the beginning the Nagas were caught in a dilemma of choices between 'autonomy and integration' with India and 'complete independence'. Although these were the two main distinct trends in which the Naga mind was sharply divided, there was little unanimity even within each of these two groups representing the two diametrically opposite views about the future of the Nagas on the eve of transfer of power. The first line of thinking was of the 'moderates' and the second were upheld by the 'extremists'. Again the extremist view was sharply divided, at least into three alternatives, namely, (*a*) to integrate the contiguous tribal areas of Naga Hills, NEFA, Manipur, and Burma to form 'British governed Crown Colony', or 'Trust Territory' in the line of 'Coupland Plan'[1] (Roychoudhury 1986); (*b*) to stay with India for a short time to establish a special relationship in order to attain experience before going for independent Nagaland; and (*c*) complete independence ab initio.

This dilemma in Naga perception about their own future and India's geopolitical interest in Naga Hills led to the Hydari Agreement (for the text of the Nine-Point Agreement, see Horam 1988) in 1947 which, up till now, has been a major bone of contention for its ambiguity—a trump card in the hands of both the opponents in the game.

However, in the initial years of the Naga movement, favourable internal as well as external environment had strengthened the extremist view. Nagas' active participation in World War II in favour of the Allied Forces brought them in close contact with the American military officials and a good reputation among the Britishers. The leaders of Naga National Council (NNC) were enthusiastic about British and American help as a good gesture for their loyalty and particularly for the services they rendered during the difficult years of war on the northeastern front. Moreover, Naga leaders were confident of mobilizing British and American opinion in their favour through the colonial administrators of Naga Hills and Baptist evangelist, both of whom sympathized the cause of the Naga independence. This political perception, it appears, had led them to reject government interpretation of Hydari Agreement and to declare independence of the Naga Hills.

The extremist Naga group consistently argued that Nagas are not Indians as they have a diametrically opposite racial, cultural, political as well as religious background. They held that the Naga Hills were never a part of India and with the cessation of British paramountcy Nagas were as free as the Indians to determine their own future. Hence, the incorporation of the Naga Hills into the Indian Union against the general will of the Naga people merely tantamount to colonial subjugation of the Naga country by the Indian state. Being the guardian of Naga interest, they were supposed to fight out any such move on the part of the Indian state. This ideology of the so-called 'Naga Nationalism' grew over a period of about thirty years since the formation of Naga Club in 1918. It got further impetus with the establishment of NNC in 1946 and was personified in Angami Zapu Phizo with his ascendancy to the post of the president of NNC in 1949. In fact, it was Phizo who roused, organized and led the Nagas in their uncompromising struggle for independence. NNC under Phizo conducted a 'plebiscite' on the question of Naga Independence in 1951 and claimed to have got overwhelming support in favour of independence. It boycotted the ADC scheme, 1952 general election, Nehru–U Nu visit to Kohima in 1953, and declared the formation of Republican Government of Free Nagaland in 1954. This movement in the face of state retaliation slipped underground and gave birth to ethnic insurgency for the first time in India with its well-defined goal, mass base, charismatic leadership, and above all, well-knit organization.

With the formation of underground Federal Government of Nagaland (FGN) in 1956, NNC found a friend in Pakistan who was ever-ready to befriend the Naga rebels in their fight against India. FGN developed contacts with Pakistan Inter-Services Intelligence (ISI), and Phizo slipped into East Pakistan, in late 1956, and then moved to West Pakistan. Bhaumik (1997) noted that from 1958, batch after batch of Naga rebels started trekking to East Pakistan for training and arms. According to Indian Military Intelligence records, at least eleven batches of Naga Federal Army recruits had been trained in East Pakistan during 1958–62. The ISI had set up bases in the Chittagong Hill Tracts for training the Naga rebels. At least 858 guerrillas were trained during this time. Besides training and arming, Pakistan also provided logistic support to Phizo's tour to England through its embassy. In 1961, Phizo became a British citizen and since then left no stone unturned to garner international support for the cause of 'Naga Independence'. Thus, the involvement of Pakistan and sympathetic attitude of some British citizens and American Baptist evangelists towards Naga insurgency have not only threatened internal security in Naga-inhabited areas, but also posed a threat to territorial integrity of the Indian state.

In order to counter the insurgent movement, the Indian state had adopted a two-pronged strategy—military response to insurgent activities and political solution to Naga aspirations. While the Indian army was fighting the insurgents in the jungles, the GoI encouraged the moderate forces among the Nagas to come forward and represent the Naga interest. During the initial years of the movement, the moderate forces remained dormant in the face of violent mass upsurge in favour of independence. Phizo tried to eliminate the political space for the moderates by purging the moderate elements in NNC hierarchy. The assassination of T. Sakhrie, an eminent moderate leader in 1955, temporarily took the wind out of sail of the moderate forces. But the departure of Phizo from Nagaland and heavy counter-violence offensive of the Indian Army paved the way for the moderates to organize the Naga people along their line of 'autonomy and integration'. The wholehearted support of the GoI to this force gave it an impetus and within a short span of time since the holding of the first meeting of the Naga People's Convention (NPC) in 1957, both the aspirations of the Nagas, that is, unification and autonomy, were met. In December 1957, Tuensang area of NEFA, predominantly inhabited by the Nagas, was merged with Naga Hills under the name of Naga Hills–Tuensang Area (NHTA) and kept as an autonomous district directly under the governor of Assam. The autonomy issue was settled in 1960 by 16-Point Agreement (for the text of the 16-Point Agreement, see Horam 1988) whereby the GoI committed to rename NHTA as Nagaland and confer statehood. Following a brief delay due to Sino-Indian border conflict in 1962, NHTA was conferred statehood in 1963. The leaders of the NPC soon formed Naga Nationalist Organization (NNO), a political party, contested assembly election held in early 1964, and came out as victorious. The moderates of Naga movement, thus, transformed into power elite and consolidated their position under the leadership of P. Shilu Ao, the first chief minister of Nagaland. It may be pointed out that NNO was formed following the model of ruling National Congress and functioned in close collaboration with the latter until its eventual merger with Congress (I) in the 1970s. Thus, cutting across the religional, cultural, and racial specificities, Naga society has been integrated with the Indian 'mainstream' along party line politics.

However, the role of violence and consequent security threats behind India's quick federalist solution of the Naga problem was not too far to see by the other aspirant groups. The implications of India's handling of the Naga issue for other communities will be taken up later. Although the creation of Nagaland could not eliminate the security threats altogether, but it had diluted the cause of 'Naga independence' to a large extent. Both the forces of integration and secession became parts of internal dynamics of Naga society.

Be that as it may, the model of integration of the tribal communities through Assam started breaking away with the separation of Nagaland. Of course, this separation was a mere recognition of the fact that Nagas were never in favour of such arrangement. The process of further disintegration of Assam started with Government of Assam's efforts to cement the segmented polity in linguistic line. We shall take up this aspect next.

Crisis of Integration through Assam Model: Relative Deprivation, Homogenization, and Security Concern

Unlike the Nagas, other hill communities voluntarily agreed to join and integrate themselves with Indian Union because of their geopolitical as well as internal social compulsions. The emerging Mizo elite of Mizo Hills, who were leading a movement for the abolition of chieftainship within their society under the banner of Mizo Union, formed in 1946, realized that it would be difficult for them to achieve their goal either under 'crown colony', the idea conceived by Coupland and supported by the colonial administrators of Mizo Hills, or 'independent' Mizoram as desired by a section of the chiefs. This internal social compulsion led the Mizo Union to join in democratic India and work in tandem with the Assam Pradesh Congress Committee (APCC) as well as

Assam government. Similarly, the emerging tribal elite of the Khasi, Jaintia, and Garo hills played a significant role in integrating their area with the Indian Union as they were increasingly identified with the mainstream national intellectual and political environment following both the Bengalis, particularly of Sylhet, and the Assamese of the Brahmaputra Valley in spite of their age-old economic ties with the plains of East Pakistan.

As it has already been pointed out, the model of integration of these tribal communities through Assam had added new dimensions to her heterogeneous population. In fact, the population composition of feudal Assam had changed completely due to territorial reorganization and large-scale, state-sponsored migration during the colonial regime. Assam's population homogeneity had been bartered against the British economic interest. There are several studies on this state-sponsored immigration in colonial Assam (Baruah 1999; Bhuyan and De 1999; Hussain 1993; Kar 1990; Weiner 1978) and we do not intend to elaborate upon it further. What is important for our purpose is the polyethnic character of the postcolonial Assam. It may not be out of context to note that while the process of unequal development within a homogeneous society leads to class cleavages, the same within a polyethnic society leads to ethnic cleavages. While the class cleavages do not pose any territorial threat in terms of separation or secession, the ethnic cleavages do, particularly when different ethnic groups are territorially concentrated. And the geopolitical location of a territory, no doubt, plays a crucial role in setting the political goal of a deprived segment. While the separatist goals are feasible irrespective of territorial location, secessionist goals are more feasible for the communities living along the international borders.

Be that as it may, the process of integration and economic development in post-independent Assam was largely embedded in interethnic competition for state privileges (Das 1996). Assamese elite, who had lost the political and economic space to British, Bengalis and Marwaris in colonial Assam, being the representative of the single largest group, took control of the state power following the Independence. In the race to gain mileage over the economic space, the state played a significant role by favouring the Assamese against other ethnic groups. The state patronage in the form of issuing license, giving contract for construction activities, issuing permits, giving order for government supply, providing jobs, financial and other benefits, etc., had put the ethnic Assamese community far ahead compared to other ethnic groups in general and tribal communities in particular. In fact, the government of Assam did not pay much attention to the development needs of the tribal communities in the hills as it considered this to be the responsibility of the central government (Nehru 1989). Moreover, following the provisions of the Sixth Schedule, ADCs, having control over the land and local resources, were functioning and were supposed to look after the development interest of the respective tribal communities. Working as an appendage to the Indian federal system, the ADCs were fully dependent on the state government for their share in the federal resources. The tribal elite being microscopic minority in state politics could hardly influence the decision-making process in their favour. This had resulted into frustration with the experiments of ADCs. The social inequality (consisting of economic, status, and political inequalities) between the ethnic Assamese and tribal communities in Assam that had resulted from the process of integration and development had soon led the tribal elite to demand separation from Assam. The outcome was the formation of Eastern India Tribal Union (EITU) in 1955 by the leaders from Khasi and Jaintia, Garo, Mikir, and Mizo hills. The EITU demanded a separate hill state for the tribals on the ground that they were being negatively discriminated by the government of Assam. However, Nehru, while visiting Shillong in 1957, tried to resolve the resentments of the tribal leaders by making an arrangement for accommodation of their interests within the framework of Assam government. Nehru was particularly anxious of the fact that while the success of ADCs would have an impact on the secessionist Naga movement, their failure might encourage others to go the Naga way (Nehru 1989). It was mainly due to Nehru's persuasion that the EITU movement remained a non-starter. But it resurfaced in 1960 under the new banner of All Party Hill Leaders' Conference (APHLC) to protest against the homogenization efforts of the Assam government by making 'Assamese' the state language of polyethnic Assam.

The clue to the opposition of Assam government's language policy, that is, making Assamese the state language of Assam, by the hill tribals, lied in Assamese-tribal relationship. In fact, Assamese society in general, and elite in particular, had been the 'normative reference group' to most of the tribal groups in Assam plains like the Bodos, Lalungs, Ravas, Karbis, Tiwas, Mishings, Deories, and so on. These groups had been keen to follow and imitate the Assamese and had aspired for long to catch up the standard of the latter by adopting their symbols particularly the language and thereby assimilating themselves with the Assamese society. In contrast to the plains tribes, the same Assamese elite had been the 'comparative reference group' to the tribes of the hills like the Mizos, Khasis, Jaintias, Garos, and so on, who used to contrast their position with respect to Assamese elite. The growing social inequalities between communities, that is, between the Assamese and different tribal groups, and the rise of Assamese elite to a hegemonic position had created a sense of relative deprivation among the tribes in general and hill tribes in particular.

Of course, the magnitude, frequency, and degree of relative deprivation had been different among the different tribal communities. The lesser the degree of assimilation, the higher was the degree of sense of relative deprivation. With the spread of Christianity, western education and culture, and consequent emergence of an elite class in the hills, both the magnitude and frequency of the sense of relative deprivation had increased manifold. As the magnitude of a sense of relative deprivation is the extent of the difference between the desired and actual situations of the person desiring it, spread of western culture in the hills had set the goals for these hill tribes far beyond the means available to them and thereby leading to a quantum jump in the magnitude of relative deprivation. With the formation of political platforms and beginning of mass mobilization under the leadership of the tribal elite for the furtherance of their political aspirations, the frequency of the sense of relative deprivation, that is, the proportion of a group who feel it had significantly gone up among the tribal communities in the hills of Assam. The degree of relative deprivation, that is, the intensity with which it is felt, had reached its zenith following the attempts to impose Assamese language on them which, they feared, would endanger their status and identity.

Thus, these twin factors, that is, social psychology of relative deprivation arising out of relative underdevelopment of the hill areas, and the perceived threat to tribal identities following the enactment of Assam Language Act, 1960, had led to the demand for separation of the hills from Assam. Initially, the APHLC demanded a hill state comprising the hill areas of Khasi, Garo, Jaintia, Mikir, and Mizo hills. Later, with the Mizos' demand for a separate state, the hill state movement grew in two directions. While the movement in Khasi, Garo, Jaintia, and Mikir hills under the leadership of the APHLC remained democratic, the same in Mizo Hills gave birth to yet another two-decade long arms struggle. As the socio-political dynamics of the emergence of Mizo insurgency was intimately linked with the language issue in Assam, an attempt is made in the next section to understand their inter linkages.

Crisis of Integration through Assam Model in Mizo Hills: Integration and Security

Like the Nagas, the Mizos were also divided on the question of joining in Indian Union following the cessation of British paramountcy. The traditional tribal elite consisting of the chiefs and their associates, who had been patronized by the colonial administrators against the commoners, favoured the idea of either joining in a British 'Crown Colony' or in Burma or to remain independent. The main objective behind this move of the traditional elite was to ensure the legitimacy of the traditional tribal authority structure which was being increasingly challenged by the Mizo Union, an organization of the commoners, which was fighting for the abolition of slavery as well as chieftainship in Mizo society. While the Mizo Union adopted the line of 'integration and autonomy', the traditional elite floated United Mizo Freedom Organization (UMFO), in 1947, as an alternative political platform. As the Mizo Union, the party of the majority commoners, had overwhelming support base, and was working in close collaboration with Assam government, the UMFO remained as a dormant secessionist force only to merge with EITU in 1957 in order to strengthen the demand for a separate hill state.

It has already been pointed out that the Mizo Union was backed by the APCC in their fight against the traditional Mizo elite since its inception. After the first general election of 1952, the Mizo Union became an official ally of Congress. Choudhury (1988) noted that the relationship between the two allies became so close that the Mizo Union lent support to the demand of greater Assam put forward by the APCC before the State Reorganisation Commission in 1954–5. But within two years this relationship deteriorated following APCC's adoption of the proposal of making Assamese the sole official language of Assam. Following the widespread resentments among the Mizos, the Mizo Union opposed this official language proposal. In retaliation, the Assam government under the leadership of B.P. Chaliha initiated a policy of tacit non-cooperation with the Mizo Union (Choudhury 1988). This non-cooperation on the part of the Assam government had made it difficult for the Mizo Union to effectively respond to the crises arising out of Mautam famine during 1959–60. The failure of the district council to address the sufferings of the famine-stricken people eventually gave birth to Mizo National Front (MNF), formed in 1960[2] under the leadership of Laldenga, and it soon became a rallying point for the secessionist forces in Mizo society.

Following the enactment of Assam Language Act in 1960, while the Mizo Union demanded a separate state for the Mizos within the Indian Union, the MNF started propaganda for secession and independence. The Assam government in its bid to use this contradiction in Mizo society in favour of its language policy backed the extremist forces. Choudhury (1988) observed:

> The MNF, from its very birth, declared 'sovereign independence' as its goal. It collected forced donations from towns and villages, raised armed volunteers and sent them for training to East Pakistan. Official records show that the Government of Assam was in the know of all these activities of the MNF, but Mr. Chaliha, in his eagerness to teach the Mizo Union a lesson, thought it expedite to pick up the secessionist MNF as his ally. He was guided by the simple logic that since the Mizo Union was demanding separation from Assam, the best course to outwit it was to encourage more extremist forces who demanded separation from India.

The MNF adopted a dual strategy in order to attain its secessionist goal. On the one hand it participated in the democratic institutions in order to enlarge its support base and on the other it started developing contacts with Pakistani authorities in East Pakistan for training and arming its cadres. In 1963 election, the MNF won 2 assembly seats and 145 seats in the village council which indicated its growing popularity.

At the same time, Laldenga and his trusted lieutenants, Sainghaka and Lalnunmawia, slipped into East Pakistan to meet Pakistani army authorities in December 1963. While returning, Laldenga and Lalnunmawia were arrested by the Border Security Force (BSF), but were released later in 1964 following the intervention of Chief Minister Chaliha. It took another two years for Laldenga to get his cadres trained and to receive arms supply from Pakistan and eventually to launch a full-scale rebellion in 1966 that lasted for two decades.

Had the APCC and Assam government stood firmly behind their trusted ally, the Mizo Union, in its hours of crisis, the historical trajectory of integration of Mizo Hills would have been different. The ripple effect of Assam's assimilationist drive had eventually ignited the growth of tribal nationalism that had, in turn, made the ITA model ineffective. While Nehru could visualize the self-defeating outcome of these efforts towards homogenization as early as in 1952 (Nehru 1989), his party colleagues in APCC did not pay any heed to his warning in their zeal to constitute a greater Assam. Thus, the obsession of Assamese elite for making Assam a 'nation-province' led them to practice hegemonistic politics in a segmented social space that eventually gave birth to insurgency in Mizoram threatening the internal security as well as territorial integrity of the Indian state.

Sino-Indian Border Conflict, Security Concern, and the Making of the NER

The Sino-Indian border conflict in 1962, some of the implications of which had already been mentioned in Chapter 1, added further security dimensions to the tribal unrest in the hills of Assam in protest against the government of Assam's homogenizing efforts on the one hand and Naga insurgency in Naga Hills, backed by Pakistan, on the other. We shall first focus on the effects of this conflict on the security environment and territorial threat to northeastern borders and then on the response of the Indian state to these challenges.

With Sino-Indian conflict resulting into close Pakistan–China relations, the NER became strategically vulnerable. The presence of China on the north and Pakistan on the east had posed a serious external security threat to the 'Chicken Neck', the corridor that passes through north Bengal and serves as lifeline between northeast and the mainland. It was believed by the strategic analysts that in the event of simultaneous thrust both by Pakistan and China towards this area, India would not be in a position to hold her NER (Bandopadhyaya 1991). It may also be noted that Pakistan's China policy was also largely informed by the security vulnerability in her eastern sector. The realization that in case of any full-scale war with India, Pakistan would not be able to hold on her eastern wing without Chinese help, led Pakistan to form strategic alliance with China against India. These dimensions, that is, strategic vulnerability of the NER against Pakistan–China alliance, and the vulnerability of East Pakistan against India, were meticulously factored into the 'Operation Gibraltar' that Pakistan launched in 1965 in order to occupy Jammu and Kashmir. Dixit has pointed out that one of the 'Pakistani strategic prediction was that India on the defensive in Jammu and Kashmir may opt to attack East Pakistan which India would consider vulnerable, and if India exercised this option, Pakistan would persuade China to attack India, thereby neutralizing the Indian threat to East Pakistan' (Dixit 1998). Zulfiqar Ali Bhutto, who later became the prime minister of Pakistan in 1971, had sent a top secret memorandum to Ayub Khan, in the middle of the 1965 war, when Pakistan was on the defensive, advocating the dismemberment of NER of India. Bhutto pleaded:

> The defence of East Pakistan would need to be closely co-ordinated with Chinese actions both in NEFA and also possibly in the regions of Nepal and Sikkim. It would be necessary to provide the Chinese with a link-up with our forces [*Pakistani forces*] in that sector. I envisage a lightning thrust across the narrow stretch of Indian territory that separates from Nepal [*the reference is to the 'Chicken's Neck' of North Bengal*]. From our point of view this would be highly desirable. It would be to the advantage of Nepal to secure its freedom from isolation by India. It would solve the problem of Sikkim and Tibet, and for us [*Pakistan*] [provide] a stranglehold over Assam, the disposition of which we can then determine.[3]

However, this is altogether different story that Lal Bahadur Shastri was far more farsighted than Ayub Khan's evil design. By directing India's thrust deep inside West Pakistan rather than opening a new front in the eastern sector, he did not provide the Chinese any scope for intervention. This is a matter of mere speculation as to what would have been the Chinese response to Pakistan's cry had India opened war in the eastern sector. Our purpose here is to highlight the strategic vulnerability of the NER about which India was well aware. The realization of this vulnerability had, in fact, informed both India's foreign policy as well as domestic policy particularly with respect to integration and development of the NER.

Soon after the 1965 Indo-Pak war, China joined hand with Pakistan in destabilizing the NER by actively patronizing the tribal insurgents. The first batch of Naga insurgent activists left for China in 1966 under the leadership of Thuingaleng Muivah (Bhaumik 1997). Between 1966 and 1978, at least nine batches of Naga militants went to China for training and arming (Bhaumik 1997). The GoI in a protest note to China, given through the Chinese charge d' Affairs on 19 June 1968, objected to the hidden external intervention (by China) into the internal affairs of India (Roychowdhury 1986). She strongly opposed to the use of Chinese propaganda media in order to 'undermine the unity and territorial integrity of India'. The protest note also informed China that India is also aware of 'growing evidence of Chinese Government's active hand in promoting subversion' particularly in Nagaland (Roychoudhury 1986). During this time the underground Naga militants circulated printed leaflets stating that Phizo had made an 'agreement with China which would invade Nagaland soon to liberate the people from the clutches of the foreigners' (read GoI) and urged the Nagas 'to have patience in their struggle for freedom' (Roychoudhury 1986). In fact this illusion created by the Naga underground think tank helped them to hold the movement in good stead for about one and half decades.

Meanwhile Pakistan successfully exploited the grievances of the Mizos and Meiteis and helped them to organize subversive activities against India. It may be noted that well before the launching of 'Operation Jericho' (1996), the MNF leader Laldenga was in touch with Pakistani authorities. The way the whole operation (revolt) was planned and organized bears the testimony of drawing the blue print by professional experts rather than a sudden outburst. The role of Pakistan behind the Mizo insurgency has been narrated in detail by Bhaumik (1996). What is important for us here is to note that Pakistan used its eastern wing as a launching pad for insurgent movements aiming to dismember the NER of India. Following the Mizo rebellion,

Pakistan started coordinating the activities of Naga, Mizo and Meitei militants so that they can jointly balkanize the NER. According to ISI papers recovered by the Indian Army after the fall of Dhaka (1971), the Pakistanis and the Chinese set up a 'Coordination Bureau' on 23 May 1969, in order to coordinate the training, arming, and funding of the insurgent movements in the NER (Bhaumik 1997). Indian intelligence agencies were well aware of this Sino-Pakistani game plan to dismember India by promoting the militant organizations of the NER. On 26 March 1970, the GoI sent a strong protest note to Pakistan condemning its (Pakistan's) attempt to promote insurgency in India's northeast in connivance with China (Roychoudhury 1986). In fact till the liberation of Bangladesh in 1971, Pakistan nurtured territorial ambition in the NER. Zulfiqar Ali Bhutto, just two years before becoming the prime minister of Pakistan, wrote in his book *The Myth of Independence*,

> [i]t would be wrong to think that Kashmir is the only dispute that divides India and Pakistan, though it is undoubtedly the most significant.... One at least is nearly as important as Kashmir dispute: That of Assam and some districts of India adjacent to East Pakistan. To these East Pakistan has very good claims, which should not have been allowed to remain quiescent. India has never ceased to take an unpleasant interest in East Pakistan and continues to support certain irredentist movements in West Pakistan. At a time when the Nagas and Mizos have revolted and thousands of Muslims have been ejected from Assam, which did not have a majority Hindu community at the time of partition, it would be wrong of Pakistan to ignore these problems. (Verghese 1996)

However, neither Ayub Khan nor Yaya Khan ever 'remained quiescent' in their covert operations to dismember the NER. The Sino-Pakistani orchestrated anti-India campaign during the late 1960s had posed such a serious threat to the security of the NER and territorial integrity of the country that even the Indian intelligence agencies became sceptical about holding the NER within the Indian Union. Desperate India found a way in the Bangladesh liberation movement to come out of this suffocative security environment. Three months before India mobilized its army to liberate East Pakistan, while Indian intelligence agencies were preparing the ground for intervention, in August 1971, P.N.

Banerji, chief of Research and Analysis Wing's (RAW) eastern division, claimed to have said in a briefing to RAW field officers at Calcutta:

> The situation in the Eastern part of the sub-continent is touch-and-go for India and Pakistan. Either we take the opportunity afforded by the Bengali revolt and break up Pakistan, and in the bargain create a friendly, secular, pro-Indian state in the region or we miss this chance and allow the Chinese and Pakistanis to intervene in North-East India at a later date, create free tribal states loyal to them and leave India a broken nation. They [Chinese and Pakistanis] are already helping the Nagas, Mizos and the Manipuri hostiles, who have each got their guerrilla units, which are giving our troops in the region much trouble. The scene may get worse, once more and more guerrillas return from China and the areas of insurgency expand beyond our capacity to control them. The only way to get India out of this worst possible predicament, when, for the first time since independence, she faces a genuine threat to her territorial integrity, is to organize the guerrilla struggle in East Pakistan with zeal and carry it to our advantage. (Bhaumik 1996)

These long quotations are cited only to focus on the strategic vulnerability of and external as well as internal security threats to the NER. We shall now turn to India's response to these threats.

Besides the fallout of India's military debacle in the Sino-Indian border conflict of 1962 on India's military doctrines, threat assessments, arms production, defence supplies, acquisition policies, foreign policy, frontier policy, and army organization, what is important to note for our purpose, is that this debacle had led to the serious criticism of Nehru's policy of integration of the hills of the NER in general and his tribal policy in particular. The border conflict had brought the NER in the limelight of national debate. The central government realized that not attending to the autonomy aspirations of different tribal/ethnic groups might further endanger the security environment in the NER. The process of taking the autonomy aspirations into cognizance that began with Naga Insurgency in mid-1950s was farther accelerated after 1962. Besides the creation of Nagaland as the sixteenth state of the Indian Union in 1963, Nehru created a Territorial Legislative Council for Manipur in the same year. It may be noted that Manipur, in spite of having a long history of organized state, was denied a responsible form of government (in place of the direct control of the centre through the chief commissioner) for all these years on flimsy 'strategic and geographical considerations' (Nehru 1986) which had resulted into large-scale political movement and social psychology of deprivation.

Although Nehru recognized the grievances of the hill tribes of Assam and intended to provide a wider politico-administrative arrangement in order to make their autonomy more meaningful, he steadfastly opposed to the demand of APHLC for separate hill state. Apart from opposition of the APCC against any further dismemberment of Assam, Nehru himself was also sceptical about the economic viability of a hill state (Trivedi 1995). He proposed a plan, which is popularly known as Nehru Plan,[4] in order to accommodate the aspirations of the hill tribes within the framework of the state of Assam which was later upheld by the Pataskar Commission (1966).[5]

But following the death of Nehru in 1964, Indo-Pak war of 1965, Mizo insurgency in 1966, and heightened security threat to the NER resulting from Sino-Pak anti-India campaign, the GoI emphasized more on satisfying the tribal/ethnic aspirations rather than looking at economic viability dimension. The Nehruvian policy of tribal integration and development having built-in isolationist overtones was replaced by a policy of progressive integration. On 13 January 1967, the GoI announced its intention to reorganize the state of Assam on a federal basis and thereby making a departure from Nehru's model of Integration through Assam (ITA). The announcement proposed:

> [T]he reorganization will be on the basis of a federal structure composed of federating units having equal status, not subordinate to one another. A limited number of essential subjects of common interest would be assigned to the regional federation, leaving the rest of the state functions to the federating units, which will have their own legislative Assemblies, council of Ministers, etc. (MHA 1966–7)

It proposed to set up a committee to work out the detail of this 'regional federation' scheme and hinted 'that at a later stage, other administrative units in the eastern region may also join this regional federation' (MHA 1966–7).

However, this grand idea of 'regional federation', having built-in promises to address both the problems of tribal/ethnic aspirations for fuller autonomy and collective action required for the common resource use and overall economic development of the NER, did not materialize.

Besides opposition from APCC, the Asoka Mehta Committee[6] which was constituted to look into the issue of reorganization of Assam also did not support the 'regional federation' proposal. It took another four years for the centre to evolve a fuller response to the twin problems of ethnic assertions in, and security predicaments of, the NER.

To digress for a moment, it may be pointed out that APCC leaders were well aware of centre's security concern behind its reorganization move. The APCC also played the same card in their bid to protect the integrity of the state of Assam. Reacting against the Centre's January announcement, APCC in its resolution adopted on 20 May 1967, observed:

> The separation of the hills and the plains would also jeopardize the security and defence of this strategic area.... Since the announcement of this proposal, fissiparous and disintegrating tendencies have extended to the other parts of the State which were so long free from any such move. Such tendencies which have since been manifesting in other sensitive parts of the country bordering China are also matters of grave concern to the country as a whole .... The proposal of a federal set up ... is pregnant with dangerous consequences, and instead of solving the problem, will give rise to further complications and accentuate the forces of further disintegration thereby creating an explosive situation in this strategically important region threatened with invasion from China and Pakistan ... the talk of separate hill state is still more dangerous to the integrity, security and defence of the country as such separatist tendency is likely to degenerate in no distant future into a movement for secession from India as is seen among a section of the people of Nagaland and the Mizo Hills. (Trivedi 1995)

Interestingly enough, as it was, the APCC resolution neither shouldered any responsibility of its inadequate understanding and ill-handling of both the Naga and Mizo problems that subsequently gave rise to demand for secessions, nor admitted the negative impacts of its policy of harmonization particularly on the hill tribes that ignited the hill-state movement in Khasi, Jaintia, and Garo hills. Instead, it projected the 'integrity of the state of Assam' as a precondition to ensure the territorial integrity of the country.

But by 1967, it was far too clear that Assam's strive to make herself a 'nation-province' had been a major destabilizing factor in the NER. The APCC resolution, devoid of any circumstantial evidence of socio-political dynamics in Assam at that point in time, could, as a result, cut little ice to bring about any appreciable change in centre's security perception.

Getting back to the issue of reorganization of Assam, on 11 September 1968, the Centre had announced a scheme indicating the creation of an 'autonomous state' within the state of Assam with a council of ministers and a legislature comprising of Khasi, Jaintia, and Garo hills, and a bill to this effect, namely, the Assam Reorganization (Meghalaya) Bill was passed in the next year (1969). But with no time, it proved to be inadequate and ad hoc. There were protracted political movements both in Tripura and Manipur for statehoods. The frustration of the Meiteis and their feeling of humiliation had already led a section to take up arms under the banner of United National Liberation Front (UNLF) demanding secession. One of the two major arguments for not acceding to the demands for statehood in these two union territories so far was their strategic geographical locations having international boundaries and stranglehold of pro-communist forces among a significant section of masses. The security concern arising out of Pakistan's territorial ambition in Tripura on the one hand and secessionist demand by the pro-communist forces under the leadership of Irabot Singh and then his followers in Manipur, and the possibility of these forces to get entangled with similar forces in Myanmar cutting across the border, appeared to have largely shaped India's response to their demands for responsible government (in the initial years of independence) and statehood.[7] This old perception faced with a dilemma in the late 1960s. Overemphasis on external territorial threat and consequent denial to redress people's aspirations for statehood had already given birth to protracted political movements leading to deteriorating internal security in both Tripura and Manipur. Moreover, with the creation of Nagaland, not only the logic behind this threat perception was considerably weakened, the second argument, that is, the redundancy of elaborate state structure involving huge economic expenses for smaller states which could no way be justified by their size of revenue (Godbole 1996) also lost its force.

A change in centre's policy in this regard, which was long overdue, was announced in parliament in 1970 (in both the monsoon and winter sessions) indicating that the central government had accepted in principle to grant statehood to Manipur, Tripura, and Meghalaya.

The announcement added that the 'details are under examination keeping in view the importance of a coordinated approach to the problems of development and security of the north eastern region' (MHA 1970–1). These 'details' were sorted out by 1971. Besides granting statehood to these three, Mizo district of Assam and, as part of pre-emptive measures, NEFA were also separated from the state of Assam and made into union territories to be known as Mizoram and Arunachal Pradesh, respectively. To give effect to this scheme of reorganization, the North-Eastern Areas (Reorganisation) Act, 1971, was enacted in the winter session (1971) of Parliament. The new states and union territories came into existence on 21 January 1972 (MHA 1971–2) leading to complete abandonment of Nehru's ITA model, after a decade of Sino-Indian border conflict.

While the GoI was working out the reorganization scheme in its bid to accommodate tribal/ethnic aspirations to checkmate the evil design of the external forces for dismemberment of the NER, political development in East Pakistan provided an unprecedented scope for Indian intervention. Two factors, which are not adequately focused in mainstream national history, that is, the geostrategic vulnerability of, and security threats to, the NER, as elaborated earlier, played no less decisive role in favour of India's intervention in East Pakistan crisis. On liberation of East Pakistan in December 1971, and subsequent emergence of friendly Bangladesh (1972), which coincided with the reorganization of the NER (1971), the over all security environments in the northeastern sector was expected to improve substantially, albeit, a hostile China remained as an external source of destabilization.

***

Thus, the approach of the Indian state towards the development of the NER, prior to 1962, was largely delineated by the Nehru's policy towards tribal development and their (tribal) integration. This policy precluded undertaking of any large-scale development projects/programmes that can impact upon the 'historical backwardness' of and structural change in, region's economy. As a result, while the country embarked upon the path of industrial development since 1956 in order to 'catch up' the west by speedily reducing the 'historical gap', the NER was kept outside the general scheme of development. In retrospect,

Nehru's warning to Bordoloi, in some other context, to leave Assam 'out of consideration' from 'general schemes of progress' (Barooah 1990), ultimately proved to be true at the end of his regime. Beside this tribal factor, the strategic location and remoteness of the region from the centre of power that influenced the security perception of the Indian state had also played a significant role in sidelining the region from the 'general scheme of progress'. This latter factor became more prominent following the 1962 Sino-Indian border conflict. The geostrategic vulnerability of the NER, arising out of Sino-Pak anti-India campaign, during 1962–71, had pointedly focused on region's security rather than on the issue of development. It was only after 1971, following the reorganization, that the Indian state thought of coordinated efforts towards the security and development of the region. The fallout of this reorganization that had significantly shaped the socio-economic and political discourses in the later years will be taken up in the Chapter 3.

Notes

1. Professor R. Coupland was a well-known British constitutional expert. He was associated with the Cripps Mission and authored a book entitled *The Future of India* (1943, London), where he dealt with the question of partition of British India in detail. The partition plan suggested by him later came to be known as Coupland Plan. He argued that the regional division of British India would be based on river basins because such a division 'corresponds with economic needs'. He suggested that India be divided into four main regions, namely, Indus, Ganges, Delta, and Deccan. The Indus basin and the Delta region were meant to be two parts of Pakistan, and the Ganges basin and the Deccan to be 'Hindu India'. His plan envisaged inclusion of both Kashmir and Punjab into one wing of Pakistan. The delta region was to include Assam, greater part of Bengal, and Sikkim. For the hill areas of Assam, Coupland had a special suggestion. He proposed that as these areas did not belong either to India or Burma, they should be grouped together into an independent political entity under the direct jurisdiction of the British Crown. This was later given the name of a 'Crown Colony' (Roychoudhury 1986).
2. Mizo National Famine Front was formed in 1960 and then two years later dropped the world 'Famine' to become Mizo National Front.
3. This extract from Bhutto's memorandum to Ayub Khan was reproduced by Stanley Wolpert in his book titled *Zulfiqar Ali Bhutto of Pakistan-His*

life and Times, cited in Dixit (1998). Emphasis added.

4. In response to the demand for a hill state by the tribal elite of Khasi, Garo, Jaintia, Mizo, and Mikir hills, Nehru proposed certain measures of change for the hill areas of Assam which was later known as the Nehru Plan. Nehru proposed 'Scottish Pattern' administrative arrangement for these areas meaning thereby that any legislation concerning them in the Assam Assembly will be passed if the members of the hill districts agree to it. He offered them 'largest autonomy within the framework of Assam'. As far as financial resource transfer is concerned, Nehru proposed a mechanism where central resources meant for the hills will be earmarked. In regard to the use of language, Nehru made it clear that the hill area will be free to use any language of their choice.
5. Pataskar Commission was constituted in 1965 to recommend a detailed scheme for reorganizing the administrative set-up of the hill areas of Assam. The three-member commission was headed by H.V. Pataskar (Chairman) and hence popularly known as Pataskar Commission. The Commission proposed to further empower the district councils and several other legal, financial, and politico-administrative changes in order to make autonomy more meaningful within the framework of the state of Assam. (For the text of the Commission's report, see Trivedi 1995.).
6. Following the rejection of the recommendations of the Pataskar Commission by the tribal elite of hill areas of Assam, the GoI constituted Asoka Mehta Committee in 1967 to consider the autonomy issue. The Committee did not favour Centre's proposal for 'regional federation'. Instead, it recommended 'maximum autonomy' for the hill areas within the framework of Assam.
7. For details see Patel's correspondence with Jairamdas Daulatram, in Sanajaoba (1988). Also see T.G. Sanjevi's (officer in Intelligence Bureau or IB) correspondence with V. Shankar (Private Secretary to the Union Minister of Home Affairs), Nehru's correspondence with Patel, and Shyama Prasad Mukherjee's letter to Patel—all reproduced in De (1998).

CHAPTER 3

Insurgency, Development, and Fragility

Having discussed the security and strategic concerns of the Indian state behind reorganization of the NER in Chapter 2, we may now, in retrospect, turn to the socio-economic and political implications of reorganization—an aspect which has not been adequately addressed by the contemporary observers on northeast affairs. Although administrators and academicians alike have focused on some of the negative implications of reorganization, the impact, however, was not of only unmixed evils without any boons.

Effects of Reorganization

To begin with the boons, first, the reorganization, that started with the grant of statehood to Nagaland in 1963 and ended with the granting the same to Meghalaya, Manipur, and Tripura on the one hand and creation of two union territories of Arunachal Pradesh and Mizoram on the other in 1972, exhibited the will and capacity of the Indian state to accommodate the aspirations of the tribal/ethnic minorities within its federal framework. This had been the response of the Indian state, positioned in a cold-war era and encircled by hostile neighbours, towards the integration of contra-cultural tribal entities/ethnic minorities. India's federal solution to this problem was marked in contradistinction with the approaches of other Asian neighbours towards similar problems—be that China's 'population transfer' to Tibet to quell the Tibetan revolt or Bangladesh's 'Muslim settlement policy' in Chittagong Hill Tracts to tame the Chakma discontent for autonomy. This federal solution to tribal/ethnic autonomy aspirations not only enabled India to pacify western nations to provide any overt support to insurgent movements but also improved her image in international forums where Pakistan was relentlessly accusing India of violating human rights. It may be interesting to note here that while Phizo visited the USA in April 1967, to garner support for Naga movement for independence, the US State Department made it clear to him (Phizo), 'Nagaland, to us, is as inseparable a part of India as Illinois or Pennsylvania are of the USA' (Roychoudhury 1986). It is, however, a different dimension that USA is alleged to have played some role in destabilizing the NER through its intelligence agencies as part of its cold-war stratagem—a common phenomenon in global diplomacy.

Second, the reorganization not only strengthened the legitimacy of Indian rule upon these hitherto 'unadministered'/'excluded' and 'partially excluded' areas in the eyes of the 'international community', it also made Indian rule legitimate among a cross section of people who are being ruled. With the creation of new states and union territories and subsequent formations of provincial governments, both the forces of integration and secession became parts of internal social dynamics in respective societies. As fighting the secessionist forces through popularly elected state governments invites less public wrath, they provided necessary smokescreen for continued anti-insurgency operation of the Indian state and its army without much social resistance.

Third, the reorganization provided a wider space for political discourses other than the politics of secessionism. Both in Nagaland and Mizoram, the conferment of statehood and union territory status, respectively, had largely weakened the cause of secessionist demands. The initial success of the moderate political elite in these two areas had been catalytic for both NNC and MNF to swallow the Shillong Accord (1975) and the 1976 Agreement, respectively. No doubt, the emergence of friendly Bangladesh in 1972 and consequent loss of safe sanctuary thereof had also played an important role behind these reconciliatory moves of the northeast insurgents.

Fourth, the creation of Meghalaya had refrained from where the tribal political elite were launching a protracted movement for hill state since 1960, to go the Naga/Mizo way. Similarly, granting the status of union territory to Arunachal Pradesh, as part of pre-emptive policy, also paid dividend. In none of them secessionist ideas could form a part of their respective internal social dynamics.

Fifth, by granting statehood to Manipur and Tripura, central government, although belatedly, recognized their rightful aspirations. The fulfilment of popular public demand for responsible government in these two states had brought an end to political unrest and widespread social psychology of political deprivation. In fact, the creation of the Nagaland state in 1963 and denial of the same to Manipur, in spite of the fact that Meiteis had a long history of state formation in contrast to the Nagas, had deeply wounded the Meitei mind. It has already been pointed out that, following the creation of Nagaland, neither the security argument nor the economic viability argument could adequately explain centre's opposition against granting statehood to Manipur and Tripura. A section of the Meities, being proud of their past, went the Naga way. They took up guns and demanded secession after eighteen long years of merger of Manipur. Indira Gandhi, through reorganization, tried to rectify this inconsistency in India's approach towards the NER. This had, to some extent, weakened the secessionist ideology in Manipur.

Sixth, the reorganization had substantially reduced the multiplicity and magnitude of linguistic, racial, and religious cleavages in the NER. The new states of Nagaland, Meghalaya, Mizoram, and Arunachal Pradesh have largely become racially as well as religiously homogeneous, although inter-tribal and tribal-nontribal cleavages still continue to persist, of course, within manageable proportion. As far as post-reorganized Assam is concerned, it is also largely relived of complex ethnic-cleavage structure.

Seventh, in order to compensate the negative impact of political reorganization on the overall economic development of the NER in terms of gainful use of common natural resources, which appeared to be problematic in post-reorganized NER with multiplicity of states and divergence of views on common interest, central government simultaneously constituted the North-Eastern Council (NEC). The NEC, constituted in 1972 following the North-Eastern Council Act (1971), was entrusted the twin task of regional development and security. The very conception of such a regional development agency with separate allotment of fund other than the plan fund of the member states was no doubt a great booster for the economy of the NER. The inclusion of both Manipur and Tripura within the NEC had made this new arrangement far wider than Nehru's ITA framework. The reorganization, therefore, sought to address all the three problems of security, integration, and development. However, whether the NEC alone is an adequate response to the problems of development of the NER or not and how effective has this agency been in realizing the stated objectives need to be evaluated.

Finally, the reorganization, by substantially reducing the political and social deprivations, particularly of the hill tribes of Assam, had significantly diminished their economic vulnerability. All the new states and union territories were given special category status in terms of plan allocation which had led to the large-scale flow of federal resources to these areas. This is, however, a different question as to why these areas, in spite of large central assistance could not make much headway.

These positive aspects of reorganization escaped the attention of those who view economic viability to be the only criterion for the creation of new states without taking the challenges of security and integration in the NER in consideration. None other than a person like Madhab Godbole (1996), who had served as private secretary to union home minister and later as union home secretary, observed:

> One can, in retrospect, seriously question the very wisdom of the creation of these small, unviable states based on narrow tribal loyalties. A concept of a typical western democracy was artificially foisted on them. As later events have shown, the hasty decisions, one after the other, to grant statehood to Meghalaya, Manipur, Tripura and Nagaland, and thereafter Arunachal Pradesh and Mizoram were disastrous mistakes.

It is, indeed surprising as to how Godbole, being one of the security managers, has missed India's security concern behind reorganization of the NER. Coming to the negative impacts, while considering the effects of reorganization on the polity of the NER, Baruah (1999) has observed, 'it energized movements for separation and discouraged a politics of accommodation'. From the foregoing discussion, it is clear that the reorganization was also a response to Assam's failure to accommodate the non-Assamese cultural aspirations in general and that of the hill tribes in particular. Thus Baruah is only partly true.

However, Baruah (1999) has rightly pointed out that 'one of the oddest effects of the reorganization of Assam is the border disputes between some of these states that mirror border disputes between countries'. Indeed, the failure of the Indian state in resolving interstate border disputes between Assam on the one hand and Arunachal Pradesh, Meghalaya, and Nagaland on the other has allowed this irritant to perpetuate for long in the NER.

As far as the success of reorganization in enhancing the security environment in the NER is concerned, Baruah (1999) feels, '[i]f the new states were attempts to contain or preempt separatist insurgencies, considering the situation today, the strategy can not exactly be called a success', meaning, thereby contrary to our observation, that there is not much qualitative change in security environment in post-reorganized NER.

However, the most important limitation of the reorganization scheme, which Baruah has preferred not to focus categorically, had been non-inclusion of any compensatory benefit for Assam. While the Indian state acceded to the separatist demands of the hill tribes out of security concern about her northeastern soft underbelly, it had not given much thought on the long-term impact of this reorganization on Assam. Hence no attempt was made in devising the split in such a way so that both sides, that is, the hill tribes and ethnic Assamese, stand to gain. For such an arrangement, the reorganization scheme should have incorporated a certain compensatory package for Assam. This could have, then, been a solace for the Assamese elite who at one point in recent history have saved the NER for India.

The role of the Assamese political elite in opposing the cabinet mission's 'grouping plan' that, if materialized, could have made Assam a part of East Pakistan, and the role of some of the congress central leadership including Nehru in favour of the very colonial plan were too vivid in the minds of the Assamese people. In fact, it was the Assamese political leadership who, by opposing to group Assam with Bengal, had in a way saved the NER for India. In post-independent India, the idea of 'greater Assam' flowed from the 1955 state Reorganization Commission's recommendations for eventual merger of Manipur and Tripura with the undivided Assam was seen as a reward to Assam for its credible role in nullifying the grouping plan. As a result, the whole process of reorganization was viewed by the Assamese elite as a machination of the centre against the interest of Assam. It not only shattered the dream of greater Assam based on Assamese sub-nationalism but also inflicted deep injury in Assamese social psyche. Although internal socio-political dynamics in Assam had ultimately made the dream for greater Assamese Assam to falter and eventually, coupled with India's security concern for the NER, led to her vivisection, the point that needs to be emphasized here is that while drawing the blueprint of reorganization no attempt was made to provide any compensatory benefits to Assam that could have acted as a heeler to the injury inflicted upon Assam. This lack of farsightedness on the part of the central government to address the injuries of Assam, while resolving the tribal problems by creating new states, has created the ground for the rise of a strong regional political force on the one hand, and a secessionist force on the other, in Assam, after seven years of reorganization. Neither the literature on anti-foreigner agitation in Assam, popularly known as Assam movement, launched under the leadership of All Assam Students Union (AASU), Asom Gana Parishad (AGP), and Assam Xahitya Xabha (AXX) combine, that lasted for long six years during 1979–85, nor the narratives on secessionist movement in Assam under the leadership of United Liberation Front of Assam (ULFA) have taken into consideration the impact of reorganization in their making.

It has already been pointed out earlier that Assam did not find any appreciable place in the national scheme of development partly due to Nehru's tribal policy, the strategic vulnerability of the region and her peripheral economic status. The colonial economic structure characterized by heavy investment in the extractive and plantation sectors hardly having any linkage—backward or forward—was allowed to continue without much effort to establish the organic link with the rest of the economy of the state. With very little central public-sector investment, the region remained exposed to the backwash effects of national development. This had made Assam unable to develop her production base along lines of comparative advantage.

As a result, except the state sector, for example, government jobs, contracts, supplies, etc., there was hardly any scope for employment. The network of administration and extension of other state services in the hills had provided a 'vent' to the job-aspiring Assamese middle class. Following the reorganization, Assam lost all these hinterlands. With no alternative openings, the Assamese middle class was drawn into a deep crisis with swelling stride of unemployment. The interethnic competition for state privileges became intense leading to the creation of a material base ripe enough to embrace the ideology of 'sons of the soil'.

Besides inflicting deep injury to the Assamese psyche and creating economic suffocation for the Assamese middle class, the reorganization also brought the interethnic competition between Assamese and Bengalis for political power and state privileges in Assam into sharp focus. The realization of the threat to the Assamese identity arising out of existence of a large Bengali population and incessant illegal emigration from Bangladesh had suddenly magnified out of proportion leading to the creation of a socio-political environment for unfolding of the anti-foreigner agitation in Assam during 1979–85.

The strong Assamese sub-national ideology articulated by the Assam movement contested the indifferent attitude of the Indian state towards the problems of identity and development of the Assamese homeland. The issues raised by the movement were real, agonizing, and reflections of collective social experience. While the leadership of the movement sought the solutions within the legal–constitutional framework, its ideology, as a by-product, like many other movements for social justice, gave birth to secessionist ideas articulated by ULFA. The rise of ULFA in Assam, the heart of the NER, undermined much of the gain in security front achieved out of reorganization.

In the next section, we shall focus on the political economy of the development process in post-reorganized the NER which has created a conducive material base for the growth and sustenance of militancy.

Reorganization and the Political Economy of Development of the NER

The measures to initiate economic development embedded in the reorganization scheme were utterly inadequate considering the historical backwardness of the region and its geographical isolation. The abandonment of the ITA model and adoption of direct and progressive integration called for far larger measures than what was envisaged in the NEC. While the NEC was entrusted with the development of intra-regional channels of communications, the fundamental task of development of communications between the region and the mainland India was not undertaken. As a result, the region till today has remained as 'far outpost', in terms of spatio-temporal distance, as earlier. Like political blueprint, there was no blueprint for economic development of the region. The security considerations have not enabled India to integrate the economies of the bordering states with nearby markets across international borders. Nor could it encourage her to integrate them by undertaking heavy public-sector investment in critical infrastructural inputs. The peripheral political and geoeconomic position of the region has made her bargaining capacity very weak compare to other regions of the country.

Interface between Social and Economic Structures

The colonial economic structure of the region having a broad-based primary sector coupled with very weak secondary sector has undergone little change even to date. This is evident from the negligible share of the manufacturing sector to the state domestic product as well as from the meagre percentage of working force engaged in this sector in all the states of the region. The developmental inputs that have been directed to this region since independence have largely been catalytic for the hypertrophic growth of the tertiary sector instead of expanding the productive base (Das 1994).

The effect of the impact of capitalist expansion in the region varies from state to state depending upon its intensity and local conditions. The result, however, is almost to create hybrid structures part being responsive to market forces, part perpetuating the features of the previously existing traditional system. Moreover, the areas where capitalistic enterprise has penetrated do not dynamically link with the other sectors, for the mass of profit it generates does not become integrated into the local economy. Both these vertical imbalances and dualistic economy are precisely the phenomena of underdevelopment of the region (Das 1994).

The state-sponsored measures of positive incentives that have been framed to heal the imperfections of the market forces are not sufficiently strong enough to outweigh the locational disadvantages and backwash effects in the regional economy. In fact, such measures like central investment subsidy, transport subsidy, tax exemption, and so on, undertaken to regulate the working of the market forces towards a desired goal could hardly motivate the industrial enterprise in this region.

The problem of underdevelopment has further been aggravated due to the coincidence of the fact that a large number of ethnic groups happen to be the inhabitants of this region who have contributed to the formation of the spatial structure of the regional economy. As a result the problem of development of this region is not only the problem of transformation of a colonial structure but also involves an upheaval task of transformation of tribal socio-economic structures having an odd number of specificities of their own (Das 1994).

Tribal land ownership pattern, systems of labour mobilization, organization of production, and systems of distribution are not yet fully responsive to the market forces. Local customs and traditions, kinship-based social relations, traditional political authorities, and other ethnocentric parameters are very much active in influencing the socio-economic base of the respective communities. As the spatial development is essentially a socio-economic process, one can not aspire to ensure economic development without any progressive change in the tribal social structures. The tribal land ownership structures and the legal as well as social barriers to the entry of outside labour in the hills of the region have contributed to the growth of group monopoly in the factor market. The idea of 'ethnic identity' has been misconstrued with the ethnic-group monopoly over the resources. Development projects that negatively affect this group monopoly and ethnic hegemony, and which dictate the socio-political terms will hardly find any socio-political sanction. While the tribal social structures rest on the ethnic group monopoly over the factor markets, the industrial development requires the elimination of all restrictions in ownership and factor mobility. Moreover, tribal societies are small in size and social fields in them are smaller. As a result, members of the society are tied by personal relationship. The smallness of the social field necessitates multiple roles to be played by the same set of people. But the medium- and large-scale economic enterprises require functionally specific roles as well as impersonal interpersonal relationship based on performance and achievement rather than on primordial loyalties. Thus, the smaller size of the society and the existence of tribal primordial loyalties stand on the way for the growth of medium- and large-scale industries in the hills of the region.

Although the concept of 'economic development' is neutral in the sense that it does not take into account the social identities of the agents, it is not this secular development perspective that the region is striving for. The question of the role of the 'sons of the soil' is always entangled with the goals of development. Economic development as a goal is desired but under the condition that it should be brought by, and directly beneficial to, the sons of the soil (Das 1998a).

Strength of the Northeastern States

The role of the non-economic political institutions, particularly those that are vital in the economic development of a society as well as in the development of modern market economy, is well established in economic literature (Borner *et al.* 2003; Weingast 1995; Weiss and Hobson 1995). Although the mainstream literature in this area refers to the role of the nation states, the same for the constituent states in a federal system in developing their respective territorial space cannot be ignored. Perhaps the neo-statist aphorism, 'strong economies require strong states' is also applicable, to a large extent, in case of constituent states in a federal system as for the union (Weiss and Hobson 1995). As it has already mentioned earlier, out of the seven states in the NER, except Assam, statehood was granted to others out of politico-security predicaments even though they do not conform the logic of economic viability. But the question is as to why even after three decades of their existence these tiny states are in no better position in terms of resource mobilization. As the relative strength of a state is usually measured in terms of its 'extractive capacity', that is, the amount of revenue it can extract, the states of the NER are, indeed, still very weak.

One of the main reasons of their abysmal performance in mobilizing resource is, perhaps, their insignificant 'penetrative power'. Penetrative power entails the 'ability of a state to reach into and directly interact with the population' (Weiss and Hobson 1995). As, unlike other states of the Indian Union, Assam, Meghalaya, Mizoram, and Tripura come under the purview of the Sixth Schedule of the Constitution, district councils having constitutional power operate as a parallel political institution occupying much of the space between the state and the people. A study on the political system of Meghalaya (Das 1998b) has shown that both the state and the district councils operate with overlapping legislative power in relation to land and people within a single socio-political field. As the Sixth Schedule has empowered the district councils to regulate and supervise the traditional political institutions at the village level, the state exercises its authority without having much direct linkage with the grassroots level.

Even in states like Arunachal Pradesh, Manipur, and Nagaland, where there are no district councils, the penetrative power is no better. In fact, there is no effective uniform legal code in relation to land and people in these states as the different tribes and sub-tribes, occupying the territorial space, are in fact governed by their respective traditions and customs.

Thus, because of their pitifully weak penetrative power, the states of NER hardly have any significant command over the resources available within their respective territorial boundary. This has largely weakened the 'extractive capacity' of these states and hence caused their failure to generate any growth impulse even under the era of state-sponsored development.

Cronyism and 'Failed State' Syndrome

Apart from these institutional and structural bottlenecks, the flow of money in the form of plan and non-plan public expenditure to these northeastern states enabled a section of people, actively engaged in various spheres of the decision-making process, to change their fortune within a short period of time. The traditional elite comprising the chiefs, *gaonburha*s (village heads), and clan leaders as well as modern political elite have been the principal beneficiaries of this transformation of the erstwhile non-monetized tribal economies into money governed market economies. A part of this money capital has been invested in the land markets emerging under ethnic monopoly. In many areas the rural rich has brought vast areas under permanent cultivation in order to establish the right of permanent possession over them. As a result, the size of the common village land, a predominant feature in the *jhum* (shifting cultivation) economy, has sharply been reduced leading to a great hardship and deprivation of the village commoners. The rising trends of concentration of cultivable land in the hands of a few and the emergence of agricultural labour in these hill economies bear the testimony to increasing vertical differentiations of the tribal communities of the NER.

The process of accumulation in the hands of a certain section of the local elite has got a great fillip with the interlocking of economic and political powers. The close correlation between these two is a generally established phenomenon in our country and more so in all the societies of northeast India. Widespread corruption, nepotism, and favouritism in every sphere of social life replaced the virtues of honesty and simplicity for which the tribals were known for long. The so-called concept of egalitarianism has reduced to a myth rather than a reality.

In all the states, a distinct pattern has emerged as far as the siphoning of public exchequer for personal benefit is concerned. Political elite, in connivance with bureaucrats, have used their high public offices to amass personal fortune either by giving various government patronages like permits, contracts, licenses, supply orders, etc., in lieu of commissions or by grabbing them for themselves through their henchmen. The rent seeking behaviour of the ruling elite is then percolated down the administrative hierarchy and thereby making mockery of the question of accountability of the public servants. The relative isolation of the region and oblivious attitude of the national media has made their job easier. Even the Indian state has tacitly approved this situation to emerge. In the bid to rally round the moderate forces behind its anti-insurgency operations, it has encouraged them to develop a stake in the system, which, it appears to have hypothesized, will then act as a necessary bulwark against secessionist forces in the region. This process, thus, has created a class of lumpen local elite. Hardly having any link to the process of socio-economic reconstruction of their respective societies, they have little commitment to the development of the region. As a result, a space has emerged in most of the societies in the NER for non-state actors to wage a war of social justice as an antithesis of the ongoing process of integration and development.

With the degeneration of political culture of the ruling elite in northeastern states, their credibility is being increasingly questioned.

They have lost moral authority to govern their respective societies. Many politicians in their bid to survive in electoral politics have struck clandestine deals with the secessionist forces—a short-cut route to power. This mutual interdependence between the constitutional and extra-constitutional forces has not only largely impaired the legitimacy of these states, it has also undermined the security objectives for which they have been created in the first place. The failure of the ruling elite to fathom out the intricacies of social change and spell out the strategy of development in definitive terms taking both the threat perceptions and aspirations of their respective societies into considerations has encouraged the victims of integration and development process to seek redress either by joining in or by organizing movements that contest the 'mainstream' political discourse.

It is important to keep these dimensions of development in the background in understanding the rise of insurgency and other social unrests in post-reorganized NER that have taken a new turn since early 1980s. Apart from these internal issues, dramatic political development in South Asia during this time has also added further force to secessionist movements in the NER. Before we take up the twin challenges of illegal migration and insurgency in the NER, a brief note on the implications of heightened cold-war tension in South Asia for the NER is in order.

Cold-war Tension and India's Northeast Soft Underbelly

The Indo-Pak relations plummeted to all-time low following the dismemberment of Pakistan in 1971 which has already been discussed in Chapter 2. The improvement in security environment in India's northeast following the emergence of friendly Bangladesh fizzled out with the assassination of Sheikh Mujibur Rahman in 1975. In order to embarrass Zia-Ur-Rehman, the martial-law administrator, who took up the reign in Bangladesh after Mujibur Rehman, and was not beyond India's suspicion, Indian external agency (RAW) took the Chakma insurgent group Shanti Bahini under its wings who were fighting for extensive autonomy in the Chittagong Hill Tracts. Since 1976, the Indian government, through its intelligence and military agencies, had trained, armed, and provided safe sanctuaries to Chakma rebels against Bangladesh throughout Indira Gandhi regime except a brief spell of Janata government during 1977–9 (Bhaumik 1996). In turn, Zia-Ur-Rahman embraced the old Pakistani open-door policy for the northeast insurgents and allowed ISI to make a come back in Bangladesh in order to step up secessionist activities in the NER. Thus, India's regime-based policy towards Bangladesh instead of country-specific policy pushed it (Bangladesh) to drift towards USA–Pakistan–China axis undermining her (India's) own interest.

Meanwhile, the Soviet intrusion into Afghanistan in 1979 flared up the cold-war tension in South Asia. India's pro-Soviet position on Afghanistan question helped further cementing of the USA–Pak axis. Large-scale economic and military assistance poured into Pakistan from the USA ostensibly to support Afghan guerrillas fighting against Soviet occupation (Kux 1993). The USA military and intelligence agencies routed this massive arms assistance through ISI. Pakistan, in turn, used ISI to foment secessionist movements in India in its desperate bid to take revenge for the loss of East Pakistan in 1971. During 1979–80, India experienced the rise of Khalistani movement in Punjab seeking its secession from the country; the sudden intensification of secessionist activities in Jammu and Kashmir; the formation of Tripura National Volunteers (TNV) seeking secession of Tripura; the formation of National Socialist Council of Nagaland (NSCN) opposing Shillong Accord signed by NNC and intensification of the struggle for Naga Independence; intensification of insurgency activities in Manipur; and Mizoram, formation of ULFA, and the launching of the anti-foreigner agitation in Assam by AASU, AGP, and AXX combined.

Besides arming Pakistan, USA's Central Intelligence Agency (CIA) had also chalked out 'Project Brahmaputra' in order to destabilize the NER. The circular issued by CIA on this project contained:

> With the agreement of the State Department, the Special Operations Research Office (SORO) of the George Washington University has asked the US outfit in India for help in conducting sociological research in the eastern states of India, including Sikkim as well as Bhutan. The aim of this research is to throw light on the public opinion in these regions to establish in what measure the present status of these states remain acceptable or whether there are indications that the formation of a new state is a current problem.

> For the conduct of this work it is necessary to mobilize the whole personnel (in the area) working in the states of West Bengal, Assam and Tripura. You may also make use of local agencies, the staff of which have opportunities of travelling in these regions.... Our organization has already carried out this type of work in a number of countries with satisfactory results, particularly in helping us to evaluate the political situation and to choose the best ways and means for our own influence there—past experience in conducting such operations shows that sociological research in India must be carried out with such discretion that we cannot be accused, on the eve of the elections, of interference in the internal affairs of the country....
>
> It has occurred in other countries that we sometimes create the impression that we have been caught with our pants down. The fact is that we do not always realize the delicacy of such works, and lack the financial and political resources to organize operations of the required quality.... In view of the importance of coming political events in India, the carrying out of this research must be conducted early. Details of the Project Brahmaputra will follow in a separate document. (Nibedon 1981)

This 'Project Brahmaputra' is believed to have some bearing for the identity, separatist and secessionist movements in the NER which unfolded with fresh impetus during the 1980s. It is held by a cross section of people from academia as well as politics that the CIA's policy of ethnic engineering is largely responsible in Balkanizing the NER. 'Project Brahmaputra' intended to initiate a movement for independent 'United States of Assam'. To achieve this goal the idea of formation of 'Seven Units Liberation Army' as mooted by bringing the existing ethnic insurgent groups under one umbrella (Jana 2001). The United States of Assam's game plan to utilize the unfulfilled development aspirations of the people of northeast against the territorial integrity of India was also articulated in political rhetoric. A member of parliament from Tripura while addressing the lower house in August 1997 observed:

> Had the Centre decided to make the investment necessary for the development of water resources and the hydroelectric potential of the North-East two decades ago, the economic scenario for [sic] the region would have been vastly different today, leaving little chance for the imperialist agencies to go ahead with their 'Operation Brahmaputra' project to destabilize the North-Eastern states and ultimately dismember the Union of India. (LSS 1997)

It may be noted that the idea of 'Project Brahmaputra' has much resemblance to that of the 'Kirkpatrick Plan'. Ms Kirkpatrick, former US ambassador to the United Nations, in a secret document submitted to the Reagan administration, advocated in favour of a policy for dismemberment of India through active US support to the separatist movements in the country. Weakening India, as it was perceived in the plan, would serve twin interests. First, the Non-Alignment Movement led by India will be weakened and it will then be easier to bring the non-aligned countries under US influence. And, second, the interest of the rival superpower (USSR) will be damaged as India was maintaining a close relationship with the former. She wrote:

> [T]he Gandhi regime pursues an anti-American policy on a number of issues, the most obvious being Afghanistan and South-East Asia, but India is not the giant it claims to be; in fact, it more aptly suggests the Chinese epithet, a paper tiger. Its weakness lies in its many unresolved domestic and international problems apart from endemic poverty. There is a noticeable growth of separatist movements, to the extent that there is a real possibility of the balkanization of India which would destroy its influence in the third world and elsewhere. Such a development, while raising a host of new problems, would undoubtedly seriously damage the interests of the Soviet Union, a traditional friend of neutralist India. (Swaminathan 1986)

Anyway, what is important for us is to note that with the climax of the cold war following Soviet intrusion in Afghanistan in December 1979, India's northeast, along with Punjab and Jammu and Kashmir, became a soft target for Pak–USA axis. The internal resentments in these areas suddenly found readily available external support from across the borders which enabled them to pose a serious threat to India's internal security and territorial integrity (Das 2002a).

It may be mentioned, by way of digression, that while Pakistan-sponsored secessionist groups were on the rise in the country during early 1980s, Soviet Union offered its support and help to India should she (India) prefer to settle the unresolved Kashmir problem militarily taking advantage of the presence of Soviet troops in Afghanistan. J.N. Dixit (1998), who was India's ambassador in Afghanistan during that time, wrote:

> A significant abortive and controversial suggestion, which came from the Soviet Union during this period, was a proposal that taking advantage of the Soviet military presence in Afghanistan, India should assume control over the whole of the state of Jammu and Kashmir and should take over areas across the line of control which was still under Pakistani occupation. The Soviet Ambassador to Afghanistan, Firkit Ahmedjanovitech Tabeev [Dixit referred to him as this, though his original name was Fikryat Akhmedzhanovich Tabeyev], was the conduit for this suggestion. He contacted me in the second half of 1982 and informed me that Soviet troops were moving into the Wakhan Corridor on the northern bank of Jammu and Kashmir. He suggested, rather picturesquely, that it was time for the two great Asian powers, the Soviet Union and India, to teach the Americans and Pakistanis a lesson. He affirmed that the Soviet Union would be supportive of any politico-military initiative which India wished to take to repossess the whole of Jammu and Kashmir and to resolve the Kashmir problem once and for all.

It is, however, a different matter that India did not step into the Soviet trap and thereby could avoid additional tension that could have arisen had she followed the Soviet proposal. Nevertheless, even after Soviet withdrawal from Afghanistan in 1989 and subsequent end of Cold War in 1991, there has not been any appreciable change in Indo–Pak hostilities. Although India has succeeded to put an end to Mizo Insurgency in 1986, TNV movement in 1988, Assam movement in 1985, Khalistan movement in 1993, the problem of integration and development in two strategic vulnerable regions, that is, Jammu and Kashmir and the NER still remain elusive. While Pakistan's territorial interest in Jammu and Kashmir has led her to sponsor low-intensity proxy war in that state which has been further aggravated with the post-1989 development in Afghanistan and also with the size of international Muslim terrorist organizations, as far as the NER is concerned, although Pakistan no longer entertains any territorial interest, she is merely utilizing the region's discontents to engage Indian army far away from Kashmir front. The region is thus being used by Pakistan as a diversionary instrument in its war against India on Kashmir front (Das 2002a).

Although China has not withdrawn its claim over Arunachal Pradesh, Ladakh, and Sikkim, it has consistently discouraged the northeast insurgent groups to cross over to its territory in search of training, arms, and sanctuary since early 1980s. But China has kept the northeast card reserved in view of India's policy towards Tibet and Tibetans. Like India's northeast, Tibet is also one of the soft spots in China. One critic of India's China Policy observed:

> The status of Tibet, and our (Indian) perception of it, has been one of the destabilizing factors in Sino-Indian relations. Publicly, the Indian government regards Tibet as an integral part of China. But in popular parlance, and in many of our actions, we do not behave as if Tibet is a part of China. For example, the Indian government had raised in the 1980s a highly paid special service unit, a [*sic*] 8000-strong commando group of Tibetans, who wake up every morning in the special camps with cries of 'Long live Dalai Lama. We shall liberate Tibet'. This commando group is still under the active supervision of the Research and Analysis Wing (RAW) and the Cabinet Secretariat. If we regard Tibet as part of China, then why is there need for maintaining such a special group? ... The Indian government has never answered this query of mine. (Swamy 2001)

This unanswered policy persuasion in regard to Tibet has encouraged China to keep both the Sino-Indian border and India's northeast questions open.

In the aftermath of Cold War, the USA has stopped directly engaging its intelligence agencies in the affairs of the Third World countries. In order to camouflage its own interest, the USA is believed to have devised a mechanism to work through, and in collaboration with, intelligence agencies/NGOs of other countries. New Delhi apprehends that in the NER, the USA is, perhaps, working through the Dutch non-governmental organizations (NGOs). In a meeting held in September 1999, to discuss the activities of Dutch NGOs in India, an official of the ministry of home affairs observed:

1. Dutch activities have suddenly increased in the region in post-cold war period. Dutch missionaries have been found active in Tripura without having any permission from the GoI. Dutch NGO, Netherlands Council on Indigenous People (NCIP), is giving support to various insurgent groups of North Eastern Region on international fora.
2. Many Dutch NGOs are directly funded by their government. It may be possible that fund flowing from the Dutch government finally trickles down to insurgent groups in North Eastern Region.

It was found that when NCIP contacted NSCN in 1993, Dutch government provided $25,000 monetary support to this NGO. This linkage of flow of fund (government–NGO–militants) has to be ascertained further.

3. It has been found that leaders of National Socialist Council of Nagaland (Isaac-Muivah) [NSCN (I-M)] faction meet the Dutch official before and after every time they meet the GoI representatives. It may be possible that the faction briefs them about the outcome of meetings. NSCN (I-M) leaders have been immunized from any restrictions to enter Netherlands on fake passport. It is not possible that the Dutch government is totally unaware of the terrorist movement, the NSCN (I-M) is leading.[1]

A background paper prepared by the IB observed that the America's claim of snapping ties with the Dutch agencies seems to be only a camouflage for continuing the covert collaboration, as the commemorative volume, CIA at 50, has an entire chapter devoted to the CIA's collaboration with the Dutch intelligence agencies. The IB paper noted that since mid-1990s, NCIP, based in The Hague, was coordinating with the Dutch foreign ministry to support the NSCN (I-M) and ULFA. The document further noted that around the same time, a Utrecht-based NGO, Land Lijke India War Group (LIW), funded by the Ministry of Development Cooperation of the Netherlands, developed links with ULFA and other militant groups in India (*The Hindustan Times* 4 April 2001).

These external factors, no doubt, need to be factored into while framing India's response towards the problems of integration and development of the NER. But they themselves do not constitute any major threat to security of the NER particularly in post-globalized era. Without any internal base to fall back upon, these external factors can hardly play any effective role in jeopardizing India's security and territorial integrity. So far, India's excessive concern with strategic vulnerability and security threat to the NER has seriously undermined the development option as a policy parameter to the problems of integration. This in turn has helped in creating a material condition that breeds and sustains insurgency and other militant movements which, then, offer the scope to the inimical external agencies to play their role (Das 2001).

Growth of Ethnic Insurgency and the Strategy of NSCN (I-M)

It has already been indicated earlier that the Naga Insurgency rooted in the process of incorporation of the Naga Hills into the Indian Union has drawn further sustenance from the aberration of the process of integration and development. The initial euphoria of achieving statehood for Naga Hills gave away to frustration and disillusionment within a decade particularly due to cronyism, growing social inequality, and widespread corruption. Although the Naga movement for independence under NNC had lost much of its appeal by the mid-1970s in the face of multidimensional changes in Naga society resulting from India's policy of progressive integration, the formation of NSCN in 1980 added a new dimension to the movement. While NNC failed to recast its ideology in the light of the changed socio-economic reality within the Naga society, the NSCN accommodated this change by including the goal of 'socialism' as one of its objectives besides the issues of Naga unification and independence. The NSCN, thus, successfully embraced the discontent of the deprived majority by setting an alternative goal before the disillusioned Nagas who hardly have any option but to respond to it positively.

An analysis of the strategy of guerrilla warfare of the NSCN, the core insurgent group, against the Indian state reveals an important dimension of the growth of ethnic insurgency in the NER. In the NSCN (I-M) view, there is hardly any internal cohesion within the Indian Union. In fact, the seeds of disintegration of the Indian Union are embedded in its formation. The utter exploitation and domination of the Indian bourgeoisie will surely pave the way for the 'discontented peoples and nationalities' to revolt against the state (NSCN 1980). While the ideological base of the Union is already on the wane, the territorial integrity of Indian state could hardly be maintained only by using force in absence of any charismatic leadership at the centre (NSCN 1985). This perception has led the ideologues of the NSCN to use the growing discontentment of the different ethnic groups against the Indian state in order to accelerate its disintegration which will in turn be helpful for the cause of Naga independence. The NSCN's logistic support to various ethnic insurgent groups in the region like the

MNF, ULFA, National Liberation Front of Tripura (NLFT), Peoples' Liberation Army (PLA), Bodo insurgent groups, and its approval of the Khalistan movement in Punjab as well as militancy in Jammu and Kashmir may well be understood if viewed from this perspective.

Both the factions of NSCN, that is, Khaplang faction, National Socialist Council of Nagaland (Khaplang) [NSCN (K)], and Isaac-Muivah faction [NSCN (I-M)], that have emerged following the split of the parent organization in 1988, as part of their strategy of guerrilla warfare, are believed to have been playing the key role behind the formation of several ethnic insurgent outfits among the different ethnic groups in the region. The NSCN (I-M), however, emerged stronger and became a major source in organising and floating militancy since 1990s. Following the surrender of A'chik Liberation Matgrik Army (ALMA), a Garo insurgent organization, on 25 October 1994, it is known that NSCN (I-M) had masterminded the whole outfit (Shira 1994). It is learnt that while staying in Dimapur, Desang M. Sangma, the general secretary of ALMA, came in contact with NSCN (I-M) activists who mooted the idea of floating an insurgent group in Garo Hills involving the disgruntled Garo youth. As a follow-up action, the ALMA was formed sometime in 1991. It appears from the narration of Silreng N. Sangma,[2] a runway ALMA recruit that the sole motive behind floating this organization was to make a quick fortune at gunpoint. It seems that the Garo youth having little experience of underground life had joined the ALMA only in lure of easy money. They were, then, trained by NSCN (I-M) activists. During its three-year existence, a series of bank robbery was jointly undertaken by ALMA and NSCN (I-M) in the Garo Hills. It is learnt that 70 per cent of the booty collected from such joint operations used to go to NSCN (I-M) as charges for its services and for arms and ammunitions while the rest 30 per cent was left with ALMA as reward for its local cover. Following the disillusionment with the hard underground life, the ALMA activists surrendered en masse in 1994.

A somewhat similar experience is also gained following the surrender of the Dimasa National Volunteers (DNV) of North Cachar Hills, Assam, as well as Hmar People's Convention (HPC) of Mizoram. The reported NSCN (I-M) links with Hynniewtrep National Liberation Council (HNLC) of Meghalaya, Karbi National Volunteers (KNV) of Karbi Anglong, Assam, and NLFT appears to be the part of the similar game plan as has been manifested in the ALMA syndrome.

It may be noted that these smaller ethnic insurgent groups are hardly the outcome of any prolong ethno-political movement. As a result, they neither have any defined political agenda nor are they rooted deep into the society. In fact, devoid of any comprehensive ideology, they act more as extortionists rather than insurgents and seemingly play in the hands of NSCN (I-M).

However, floating of such smaller ethnic insurgent groups serves two broad purposes for NSCN (I-M). First, it opens up multiple fronts for the counter-insurgency agencies and keeps them busy elsewhere rather than concentrating in the strongholds of the core insurgent group.

Second, it helps the core insurgent group to mobilize additional resources from areas beyond its sphere of influence as well as provides the necessary cover-ups for its operations in all together different ethno-social milieu.

Besides these two purposes, the act of engineering insurgent movements among the different ethnic groups also fits into the NSCN (I-M) strategy to turn its own war with the Indian state into a war of the nationalities of the region. The strategic importance of the Indo-Myanmar border area, favourable topography for guerrilla warfare, existence of ethnic affinities across the border, the long experience of underground movement, and well-developed rapport with foreign agencies have made NSCN (I-M) such a hegemonic power that it has become a rallying point for most of the insurgent groups. The formation of United Liberation Front of the Seven Sisters (ULFS), a common platform of different ethnic insurgent groups, in 1993 under the leadership of NSCN (I-M) seems to be a pointer in this regard. As the ULFS remained as a non-starter, the NSCN (I-M) made another effort in 1994 by forming the Self Defence United Front of South East Asian Himalayan Region with twenty three different insurgent groups operating in the region as well as in Myanmar. Thus the Naga insurgency in general and NSCN (I-M) in particular has long been a constant source of inspiration and catalytic agent for the rise and proliferation of insurgent movements among the different ethnic groups in the region.

It may be noted that skepticism of NSCN (I-M) about the sustenance of multiethnic India is akin to that of the western countries particularly of the UK and the USA. During 1950s and 1960s, the idea that India will dismember along ethnic lines was predominant among the western political think tanks. Moreover, the strategy of NSCN (I-M) to convert its own war against the Indian state into the war of nationalities of the region resembles the objectives of CIA's project 'Operation Brahmaputra'. The role NSCN (I-M) in training, arming, organizing, and coordinating ethnic insurgencies in the NER seems to be indicative of the fact that it is working as a conduit for foreign forces that seek to undermine the security and territorial integrity of the country. The facts that the NSCN (I-M) leadership keeps close contact with Pakistani authorities and operates from Bangkok, where CIA has an operational headquarter, further lend support to this hypothesis. As a result, there is no wonder that containment of NSCN (I-M) has formed an important element of India's anti-insurgency policy in the NER.

Failure of Democratic Conflict Resolution Mechanism and Insurgency

Insurgency has become a political mode of communication in the hands of the small tribal/ethnic groups in the NER. As each of the seven northeastern states contains numerous smaller tribal/ethnic communities having their respective socio-cultural specificities, aspirations of all these groups cannot be addressed with equal justice within the politico-administrative structure run on majoritarian principle. In parliamentary democracy, political parties articulate the grievances of various segments of the people. Non-fulfilment of the aspirations under a particular regime may lead to change in regime facilitating new initiative towards their solution. But this built-in conflict resolution mechanism in democratic process is largely biased in favour of the majority group in a multiethnic society. The smaller communities, not being in a position to influence the outcome of political verdict, attract less attention from the competing political parties. As a result, smaller communities often find themselves left in political vacuum which, in turn, compels them to play the role of a political community articulating their respective group interest. As these communities cannot impact upon the democratic decision-making due to their meagre number, they can hardly sensitize the institutions of democracy about their aspirations and anxieties particularly if their solutions call for attention of the central government. Faced with this predicament of democratic conflict resolution mechanism, smaller communities often find it useful to adopt militancy as an element of their political strategy. Many of the autonomy and identity movements in the NER have resorted to such tactics by promoting an 'armed wing' alongside the democratic instruments of struggle. Be it the Bodos, or Hmars or Kukis or Reangs (Brus), in all cases a similar pattern of combining the means of democratic protest with doses of militancy may be noted. With the presence of active foreign powers across the borders, these militant wings, in no time, transform themselves into insurgent groups. With gun in hand, they, then, as it has happened in many a cases, overpower their respective political wings and dictate the future course of the movements keeping the interest of their patrons in mind (Das 2005a).

However, it is not possible to generalize the course of various ethno-social movements in the NER. Neither do they follow a unilateral path, nor do they exhibit a completely different strategy. In fact each movement reinforces the other depending upon one's reading of the other. As the interest of different ethnic groups is often competitive rather than complementary, actions of one group bring some other groups into being. The inability of the northeastern states to fathom out a structure of interethnic relationship in order to harmonize their respective social space has further encouraged various groups to devise their own institutional mechanism that can combat the threats and advance the respective group interests. In the process the secular social space is getting marginalized and people are being increasingly polarized along ethnic lines (Das 2006a).

Ethnic identities rooted in primordial loyalties are essentially exclusive in nature. The exclusivist principle working through deductive process is leading to further reduction of ethnic boundaries. This has not only resulted into the creation of many new identities but has also made each of them powerless in relation to the democratic structure which in turn has encouraged them to adopt militancy as a political strategy.

Electoral Politics, Incentives, and Insurgency

Besides the majoritarian political framework, the practice of power politics by different parliamentary forces also contributes to the growth and perpetuation of violent ethnic movements in the NER. A close observation of the contemporary political situation in the NER reveals the interlinkages between insurgent activities and electoral politics. The tribal insurgency in Tripura resulting from their relative backwardness and threat to their identity arising out of large-scale Bengali immigration has profitably been used by the parliamentary forces for electoral gains. It has been alleged that the genocide committed by the TNV activists before the 1988 assembly election at the behest of the Congress (I)–Tripura Upajati Juba Samiti (TUJS) combine opposition paved the way for the latter to power (Das 1997). The signing of an accord between the Congress (I) government at the centre and TNV, immediately after the election, to accommodate the interest of the latter is often cited as an indication of the clandestine understanding between the two. Similarly, the massacre committed by the All Tripura Tribal Force (ATTF) activists on the eve of 1993 election is believed to have helped the CPI (M)-led Left Front to make a come back to power (Das 1997). It is reported that while the ATTF and the Tribal Youth Force (TYF) have been floated by the Gana Mukti Parishad, a Communist Party of India (Marxist) [CPI(M)] tribal wing, the Tripura Tribal Volunteer Force (TTVF), the Tripura Tribal Development Force (TTDF), and the Sangkrak enjoy clandestine support from the TUJS, a Congress (I) ally (Das 1997).

Thus, it appears that even the mainstream political parties, in their bid to capture the state power, not only patronize the insurgent groups, more often than not, also float such organizations to carry out subversive missions in order to destabilize the existing regime. After assuming power, they stage a surrender making drama with much fanfare by granting a general amnesty to all militant activists along with provisions for economic rehabilitation. It may be mentioned here that immediately after the assumption in office by the CPI(M)-led Left Front in April 1993, about 2,000 ATTF activists surrendered before the government on 9 September 1993. A similar incident had also taken place during the Left rule earlier while the activists of All Tripura People's Liberation Organization (ATPLO) led by Binanda Jamatia came overground. This, however, serves two main purposes for the mentors simultaneously. First, it helps them to make a come back to the seat of power by tarnishing the image of the ruling political force. Second, the surrender-making drama boosts up the political image of the hitherto opposition forces, now in power. As if it is their credit that they have brought normalcy and peace in the turbulent socio-political environment. For the insurgent activists, it simply pays them in terms of government job, license, permits, and other benefits on return to mainstream which would have been almost impossible to get otherwise.

But, in no time, the dislodged political forces, now in opposition, play the same game that gives birth to new militant organizations only to carry out their crusade against the forces in power. Although this observation is an over simplification of the complex ground realities and hard evidence to substantiate such a thesis explaining the power politics as a catalytic agent for thriving insurgent activities in the tiny state of Tripura will hardly be available, this impressionistic observation offers a plausible explanation of the insurgency phenomenon in Tripura characterized by streams of surrender and dissolution of some only to be replaced by other insurgent groups. The hypothesis suggesting a linkage between the dynamics of bipolar electoral democracy and insurgency in Tripura gets further strengthened due to the fact that as soon as the principal rivals in the state politics, that is, CPI(M) and Congress (I) became ally at the centre following the 14th Lok Sabha election in 1994, the intensity of insurgent activities suddenly came to a low ebb. In fact, insurgent groups have suddenly melted down and normalcy restored in state politics in no time.

However, the interlinkages between electoral politics and insurgency do not follow any definite pattern everywhere in the NER. An opposite syndrome may also be noticed elsewhere particularly in Assam and Nagaland where major insurgent groups play tricks in changing political regimes to suit their interests. In Manipur, the power elite maintain close relations with different insurgent groups at individual levels. They resemble the African war-lords who maintain personal war-troops. The larger the troop, with which a person associates, the greater is its striking power, the stronger becomes his claim for ministerial portfolio. The bigger the portfolio, the greater is the capacity of that person to shield the troop from state/army onslaughts and to dole out crumbs of power.

The close nexus between the power elite and insurgents in Manipur is well known to all sections of people as reports on this frequently keep on appearing in print media. Recently, army has implicated the ex-chief minister, Mr Nipamacha Singh and former Assembly Speaker L. Chandramani Singh for donating huge sums to UNLF. Each of them, it is alleged, has paid Rs 1 lakh and Rs 2 lakh, respectively. This nexus is so strong in Manipur that any effort to break it invites political instability. As soon as the Koijam government sacked six of its ministers having links with the insurgent groups on 14 April 2001, his government has been immediately voted out of power following the overnight change in coalition chemistry. There are innumerable evidences of patronage of the insurgent groups by the politicians in Manipur (Barua 2008).

This nexus draws further life because of the fact that mainstream political parties, having hardly any social base, work through the local political formations. The local politicians, in turn, by using the contradictions of national politics, form support bases of one or the other mainstream political party which provides them necessary safeguards against their clandestine deals with the insurgent groups.

The ruling elite of the northeastern states also sometimes seems to extend tacit support to the insurgent groups in order to keep them alive which is then used as a ploy in bargaining for more central assistance. As the expenditure incurred on counter- insurgency operations, like other secret services, remains beyond the audit surveillance, there is hardly any way to make the ruling elite accountable even if a large share of such fund is siphoned off for personal gratification. In the context of high level of corruption and nepotism prevalent in all the states of northeast, the motive of attracting additional central assistance may also be another plausible factor behind the perpetuation of certain insurgent movements in the region.

Besides these direct economic incentives, the ruling elite sometimes also seem to allow insurgent movements to perpetuate in order to make themselves indispensable in state politics as well as to secure their positions. It may be recalled that while the possibility of negotiated settlement of the ULFA movement became bright in the early 1990s and the stage for such a settlement was ready following several round of talks between the ULFA leadership and the central government, the ruling elite in Assam headed by Hiteswar Saikia reported to have sabotaged this move (Das 1997). Perhaps, they feared that such a settlement might oust them from power as it had happened earlier in case of Assam Accord in 1985[3]and Mizoram

Accord in 1986.[4] It is widely believed that had an accord been signed with the undivided ULFA, the insurgency problem in Assam would have been solved á la Mizoram. The ruling elite in Assam, instead of complete political solution, engineered a vertical split within ULFA that ultimately brought Surrendered United Liberation Front of Assam (SULFA) into existence and followed the policy of divide and rule in order to secure their own political fortune. They brought the movement down to such a level so that it remains under control but did not put an end to it. They allowed it to perpetuate perhaps to make themselves indispensable in state politics.

Intensity, Spread, and Proliferation of Ethnic Militancy

As has already been stated, India's first ethnic insurgency began in Naga Hills during the mid-1950s. After a decade, it engulfed Mizo Hills with MNF rebellion in 1966 that lasted for two decades. By the end of 1960s, ethnic insurgency spread among the Meities of Manipur valley. Tripura tribals followed suit with the formation of TNV in 1979. With the birth of ULFA (in 1979) and its growth (since 1985), and the formation of Bodo Security Force (BdSF), the Brahmaputra Valley, the heart land of the NER, also drawn into ethnic war. Thus, within three decades since the beginning of Naga insurgency, the virus has spread all along the length and breath of the region. While the Naga insurgency is primarily based on the racial ground and has sprung up from the attempt of incorporation of Naga Hills into the Indian Union, ethnic insurgency in Manipur, Mizoram, and Assam (led by ULFA) have largely been the outcome of utter economic underdevelopment. The tribal insurgency in Tripura has been the response against the relative deprivation of the tribals and their identity crises caused by the large-scale Bengali immigration. The Bodo insurgency in Assam has resulted from the 'domino effect' of identity assertion and relative deprivation that has led many a smaller group to embrace militancy as a political strategy. Although Assam, Manipur, and Nagaland are now the centre stage of insurgent activities, Meghalaya is being used as a safe heaven by the region's extremist groups and both the Khasi and Garo insurgent groups are acting as conduits for others. Arunachal Pradesh particularly its eastern segment is under the active influence of different Naga insurgent groups. Mizoram, even after the end of Mizo insurgency in 1986, was faced with fresh Hmar and Reang insurgent activities. Thus, all the seven northeastern states are, by and large, affected by the phenomenon of ethnic insurgency.

The formation of Kamatapur Liberation Organisation (KLO) and Gorkha Liberation Organisation (GLO) in the plains and hills of North Bengal respectively and their reported links with the insurgent groups of northeast (Banerjee 2005) indicate that ethnic insurgency is gradually transcending the border of the NER and penetrating the heartland. Once these organizations establish links with Maoist Communist Centre (MCC) active in Bihar, and further down South with People's War Group (PWG), active in Andhra Pradesh, both of whom support the cause of self-determination of all ethnic groups, and then the northeast will be able to imprint its own image within India's heartland. However, with the collapse of the Liberation Tigers of Tamil Eelam (LTTE), which was believed to be an important source of supply of arms in the region, the link to the further south has received a jolt.

Ethnic insurgency in the northeast, besides posing a challenge even beyond the region, is fast acquiring a South Asian as well as Southeast Asian status. Apart from Bangladesh, which has long been used by the northeast insurgents as safe sanctuary, the territory of Bhutan is also being increasingly used. Since 1991, following large-scale army operation in Assam, ULFA and National Democratic Front of Bodoland (NDFB) established a few bases inside Bhutan. After the AL's return to power in Bangladesh in 1996, which is perceived to be pro-Indian, ULFA and NDFB had shifted many of their training camps inside the deep forests of south-eastern Bhutan bordering Assam. They believed to have developed good rapport with some of the Bhutanese officials who extended logistic support to their endeavour. In spite of the fact that Bhutan had noticed their presence in its territory in 1994, as has claimed by the government of Bhutan, it is only after four years in 1998 that Bhutan initiated talks with ULFA in order to persuade the latter to leave Bhutan. It appears either Bhutan had tacit support in hosting the northeast insurgents at least in initial years or was too panicked to oppose their activities. It was only after mounting pressure from Indian government that Bhutan had officially turned its back towards these insurgent groups and explicitly stated its security concern caused by their presence. Although Bhutan had flushed out the insurgent groups from its territory in December 2003, through a coordinated anti-insurgency operation with the Indian army, Bodo militants are still active along the Indo-Bhutan border.

Besides the two South Asian countries of Bangladesh and Bhutan, northeast insurgents have also well entrenched into Myanmar territory, our Southeast Asian neighbour. In fact, the problem of ethnic insurgency is far more complex in Myanmar than any of its Asian counterparts. Beginning with the Karen nationalist movement under the leadership of Karen National Union in 1949, the ethnic insurgency had swiftly made in road among the Mons, Karennis, Paos, Kachins, Rakhines (Arakans), Chins, Kayahs, Shans, Palaungs, Wars, Nagas, Lahus, Kokangs, Danus, Akhas, and Rohingyas. These ethnic minorities occupy about 40 per cent of Myanmar's total land area where insurgent movements have remained firmly entrenched. Most of these ethnic national movements have their own well-organized armed groups that control their respective 'liberated zones' where the writ of the Myanmar regimes hardly work. Until early 1980s, China used to patronize many of them either directly or through the Communist Party of Burma. The 'liberated zones' under the control of the various ethnic militia had long been used by the northeast insurgents particularly by the Nagas and Meiteis for setting their camps and as corridors to reach China. The Karen National Union's base at Mannerplaw in South Myanmar and Kachin Independence Organisation's (KIO) headquarters at Pajao on the Chinese border had become important liaison posts for insurgent forces in Myanmar where a number of nationalist armies were trained to fight against Myanmar's army. Northeastern insurgent groups like NSCN, ULFA, FGN, and PLA were also sustained by KIO, in terms of providing safe sanctuary, arms training, and arms supply. In fact, since independence, Myanmar remained engaged in a perpetual state of strife. The 'endless state of war' and the growth of 'narco-terrorism' in Myanmar have important ramifications for the internal security of the NER.

The ethnic insurgency in the northeast has, thus, acquired a global dimension directly involving Pakistan, Bangladesh, Bhutan, and Myanmar. With the ISI fast spreading its network, Nepal is also being drawn into the battle indirectly. As the area of operation of the various northeast insurgent groups is far wider than that of Indian Army, Indian state has to evolve an effective diplomatic strategy in order to work through the government of neighbouring countries.

Besides the spread, the intensity of insurgent activities in the NER particularly in the four states of Assam, Manipur, Nagaland, and Tripura, where insurgent groups are most active, has also exhibited a sharp rise since early 1990s. Indicators like number of violent incidents committed by the insurgent groups, number of arrests of the insurgent activists, number of surrenders, number of insurgent activists killed, number of persons killed by the insurgents, etc., which, inter alia, are generally used to measure the intensity, are not out of doubt. As statistics relating to these indices are recorded by various security agencies and classification of these events under various heads is very often done on the basis of intuition and pro-state bias, there remains enough room for subjective judgment. Moreover, these statistics without details hardly lend themselves to researcher's verifications. Besides their limitations, these statistics are not easily available, even while available, they very often lack in continuity and comparability.

Table 3.1 represents state-wise number of incidents of insurgency that have taken place since 1985. Statistics presented in Table 3.1 are collected from various issues of the annual reports of the ministry of home affairs. These statistics are neither exhaustive nor unique. Moreover they suffer from state-centric biases. Nonetheless, one can form an idea of the intensity of insurgent activities in the region over the years. The statistics show a clear trend of rise in insurgency-related incidents from the mid-1990s. During 2002–6, for which we have complete information, 9,633 insurgency-related incidents have taken place in the NER, which means on an average, about four incidents per day.

Table 3.2 represents state-wise number of insurgency-related deaths in the region. During the last seventeen years, from 1992 to 2008, 18,258 people of all categories including the militants, security forces, and civilians have died in the region. This indicates on an average 1,074 deaths every year and about 3 deaths per day.

If the number of death is taken as the measure of intensity of insurgency, then Assam is the worst affected state having the highest number of death toll during the last seventeen years (1992–2008), followed by Manipur, Tripura, and Nagaland.

Table 3.1: Incidents of Insurgency in the NER

Year	*AP*	*Assam*	*Manipur*	*Meghalaya*	*Mizoram*	*Nagaland*	*Tripura*	*Total*
1985	–	–	–	–	–	–	72	72
1986	–	–	–	–	–	–	47	47
1987	–	–	–	–	–	31	42	73
1988	–	11	–	–	–	21	–	32
1989	–	19	–	–	–	–	–	19
1990	–	42	–	–	–	–	–	42
1991	–	137	135	–	–	32	–	304
1992	–	278	141	–	–	34	–	453
1993	NF	NF	NF	NF	NF	NF	NF	
1994	NF	NF	NF	NF	NF	NF	NF	
1995	NF	NF	NF	NF	NF	NF	NF	
1996	–	–	318	–	–	246	246	810
1997	–	315	288	–	–	261	391	1,255
1998	–	427	425	–	–	380	303	1,535
1999	–	735	255	–	–	202	568	1,760
2000	–	447	281	–	–	294	614	1,636

(*Continued*)

(Continued)

Year	*AP*	*Assam*	*Manipur*	*Meghalaya*	*Mizoram*	*Nagaland*	*Tripura*	*Total*
2001	NF	NF	NF	NF	NF	NF	NF	
2002	54	412	268	84	1	208	292	1,319
2003	50	358	243	85	3	199	394	1,332
2004	41	267	478	47	3	186	212	1,234
2005	32	398	554	37	4	192	115	1,332
2006	16	413	498	38	5	309	87	1,366
2007	35	474	584	28	2	272	94	1,489
2008	28	387	740	16	1	321	68	1,561
Total	256	5,120	5,208	335	19	3,188	3,545	17,671

Source: *Annual Report*, various issues, MHA, GoI.

Note: NF stands for Not Found.

Table 3.2 Total Number of Civilians, Security Forces, and Terrorists Killed in the NER

Year	*Assam*[1]	*Manipur*[2]	*Meghalaya*[3]	*Nagaland*[4]	*Tripura*[5]	*Total*
1992	133	165	0	96	98	492
1993	131	423	0	173	183	910
1994	271	350	4	192	238	1,055
1995	270	321	7	213	257	1,068
1996	451	275	7	304	189	1,226
1997	537	495	4	360	274	1,670
1998	783	244	20	112	265	1,424
1999	503	231	22	148	303	1,207
2000	758	246	36	101	514	1,655
2001	606	256	40	103	312	1,317
2002	445	190	64	36	175	910
2003	505	198	58	37	295	1,093
2004	354	218	35	58	167	832
2005	242	331	29	40	73	715
2006	174	285	24	92	60	635
2007	437	408	18	108	36	1,007
2008	373	485	12	145	27	1,042
Total	6,973	5,121	380	2,318	3,466	18,258

Sources:

[1] http://www.satp.org/satporgtp/countries/india/states/assam/data_sheets/insurgency_related_killings.htm (accessed on 12 December 2009).

[2] http://www.satp.org/satporgtp/countries/india/states/manipur/data_sheets/insurgency_related_killings.htm (accessed on 12 December 2009).

[3] http://www.satp.org/satporgtp/countries/india/states/Meghalaya/data_sheets/insurgency_related_killings.htm (accessed on 12 December 2009).

[4] http://www.satp.org/satporgtp/countries/india/states/nagaland/data_sheets/insurgency_related_killings.htm (accessed on 12 December 2009).

[5] http://www.satp.org/satporgtp/countries/india/states/tripura/data_sheets/insurgency_related_killings.htm (accessed on 12 December 2009).

Although insurgency in Nagaland is quite old in terms of duration, the intensity of insurgent activities is very high in Assam, Manipur, and Tripura compared to that of Nagaland. Annual figure for the loss of human lives is substantially higher in Assam, Manipur, and Tripura compared to that of Nagaland. This is because of the fact that in Tripura and partially in Assam ethnic insurgencies are largely rooted in interethnic rivalries. While in Tripura, tribal insurgent groups aim at driving out the migrant Bengalis, in Assam the Bodo insurgent groups frequently launch ethnic cleansing drive in order to oust the other ethnic minorities from the 'promised land' of the Bodos. Similarly, Nagas in North Cachar Hills are trying to eliminate the Dimasas in order to strengthen the claim for the merger of these hill areas with Nagaland. There is wide-spread believe that NSCN (I-M) is instigating the Zemi Nagas living in North Cachar Hills to go for all out cleansing of the Dimasas. In fact interethnic rivalries for territorial control often lead ethnic armies to resort to ethnic cleansing. In case of Manipur, Meitei insurgent groups often resort to mass killing of the 'outsiders' (read Indians) to take revenge against the killing of the Meitei insurgents by the security forces.

One of the reasons behind this sudden rise in insurgent activities has been the fast proliferation of small arms in the NER since the early 1990s. Following Soviet withdrawal from Afghanistan in 1989, the huge quantity of sophisticated weapons that the USA made available to the ISI, Talibans, and other Afghan guerrilla groups during 1979–89 became a major source of supply for the insurgent groups in India. Through ISI network, it is believed, a part of this stockpile has landed in the hands of the militants in Jammu and Kashmir, Punjab, and the northeast.

However, for the northeast insurgent groups, the major source of supply of arms and ammunition is the so called 'golden triangle' consisting of Combodia, Thiland, and Myanmar. It is believed by the intelligence agencies that about 80 per cent of arms procured by the northeast insurgent groups originate from this triangle.

By way of digression, it may be recalled that as part of its policy of containment of communism in Southeast Asia, US has dumped huge arms and ammunitions in (South) Vietnam during 1950–75, and Cambodia and Thailand during 1969–91. All along Soviet Union backed Vietnam's occupation of Cambodia (1975–89), the USA, China, and other western powers provided economic and military assistance to Khmer Rouge leader Pol Pot. In fact, like Afghanistan, Cambodia was also bitterly caught into the super power rivalries during the cold-war era that had completely shattered its social fabric. However, with the withdrawal of Vietnam from Cambodia in 1989 and return of normalcy following the signing of 1991 agreement, Cambodia found herself burdened with huge illegal arms that eventually led to the growth of clandestine 'arms market'.

The growth of 'arms market' in India's northwest (Afghanistan) and northeast (Cambodia) neighbourhoods during the early 1990s has a tremendous implication for the country's internal security. As far as the procurement of arms by the northeast insurgent groups is concerned, LTTE used to play an important role. The LTTE, having a strong command over the sea routes, used to ship arms from Cambodia to Cox's Bazar, Bangladesh's southernmost tip. Then from Cox's Bazar, these arms used to enter into Myanmar and the NER. In fact, the long porous borders between the NER and Myanmar as well as between the NER and Bangladesh provide endless unmanned entry points either through dense forests and high hills or through riverine routes for sneaking in arms in the region by the insurgent groups.

Although it is not possible to quantify the volume of arms stock pile in the hands of different insurgent groups in the NER, the magnitude of the problem may roughly be inferred from the recovery of arms by security forces from different groups. Dasgupta (2001) has reported that during the last five years (from 1995 to 3 April 2000) security forces have recovered a total of 1,075 arms including rocket launchers (4), LMGs (11), SLRs (16), AK series of rifles (90), other rifles (106), carbine/stengun (91), pistol/rivolver (578), DBBL/SBBL (99), and others (79) from different insurgent outfits in Assam alone. She has also computed, from police file, a total of 4,171 arms recovered only from ULFA in Assam during the last decade (from 1991 to April 2000) consisting of 961 pistols/revolvers, 223 CM pistols/rivolvers/guns, 345 rifles including AK series, 145 stengun/carbine, 1 rocket launcher, 2 live rockets, 14 LMGs/UMGs, 1 machine gun, 2,479 shot guns, and others.

Indeed, this information only shows the tip of the iceberg. The easy availability of arms in the NER's neighbourhood has not only compounded the conflict resolution mechanism but has also led to the proliferation of ethnic insurgencies in the region. Easy access to arms is certain to aggravate social conflict which could have otherwise been resolved through negotiations. Proliferation of small arms in the region encourages discontent groups to adopt armed struggle as political strategy rather than adopting any democratic means. This also encourages 'armed gangs' to grow and flourish who use their guns to make fortunes.

In Tripura, while the first tribal insurgency ended in 1988 with the surrender of TNV, but since then within a span of six years (1988–95) at least more than a dozen of new insurgent groups came into being. Conflicting interethnic interest has, thereafter, given birth to United Bengali Liberation Force (UBLF) and Bru Liberation Army (BLA). Of course, all the groups are not equally active. There are some organizations that only exist by name without any serious striking power. Some work as conduits for the more powerful groups. Some are essentially armed extortionist gangs masquerading as ethnic revolutionaries. Similar is the case of Manipur where as per the last counts as many as seventy insurgent groups operate. In Assam there are at least seven active groups and more than a dozen, although insignificant, minority (Muslim) militant groups. Nagaland, Meghalaya, and Mizoram are having at least five, two, and two active insurgent groups, respectively.

***

In fact the proliferation of arms in the NER coupled with the long existence of Naga insurgency, open international borders, favourable socio-political milieu across the border have resulted in a situation where discontents among the various ethnic groups arising out of various contexts, for example, economic deprivation, conflicting interethnic interest, underdevelopment, identity assertion, autonomy aspirations, easily transform themselves into ethnic insurgency. Unlike civil wars in Africa, where greed acts as the driving force, grievance is the primary driving force for militancy in the NER. The fast proliferation of militancy in the NER and its rising intensity have created a situation of fragility where democracy works only as a façade and most of the subunit level governments have failed to ensure human security. The adverse impact of insurgency on economic development and how the interplay between insecurity and underdevelopment has led to the emergence of a conflict trap in the NER will be discussed in Chapter 4.

Notes

1. See http//www.tehelka.com reported from the minutes of the meeting at the MHA, held on 29 September 1999, to discuss the activities of Dutch NGOs in India.
2. Silreng confessed that he and three of his friends had received a sum of Rs 2,000 each for joining ALMA. But as soon as they were taken to ALMA camp at Damal A'sim, the money was taken back. Having realized the ALMA trick, Silreng managed to flee.
3. Following the Assam Accord between the AGP and the GoI, Hiteswar Saikia-led Congress (I) government in Assam had to give way to AGP-led government.
4. Following the Mizo Accord, Laldenga-led MNF came to power in Mizoram.

CHAPTER 4

Interlinkages between Security and Development

Having discussed as to how the development interest of the NER has become hostage to the state-centric security perception of the Indian state prior to the collapse of bipolarity in Chapter 1, and how the external security concerns have shaped the internal political reorganization of the region in Chapter 2 as well as the political economy of growth of insurgency in Chapter 3, we now turn to focus on the interlinkages between security and development in this chapter.

Security and Development: The Economic Costs of Insurgency

There exists a two-way linkage between insurgency and economic development. Let us first discuss the impact of insurgency on economic development and the channels through which the former influences the latter. Insurgent or militant political movements use violence as a strategic tool in order to achieve their goals. It has already been discussed in Chapter 3 as to why minority ethnic groups in a multiethnic society adopt violence as a political strategy. As these groups cannot influence the democratic decision-making process in a number-based electoral democratic system, they often resort to violence to draw the attention of the political authority. The acts of violence degenerate the security environment which in turn creates roadblocks for the smooth operation of the institution of market. Entrepreneurs, investors, producers, and consumers have to factor into the social and political violence in their decision-making. As insecurity raises the risk factor, business premium goes up for all sorts of economic activities. As a result, not only price level shoots up which denies the insurgent-prone areas to grow along the lines of their respective comparative advantage, but also encourages the businesses to relocate elsewhere. In fact there are a number of channels through which deteriorating security environment impacts upon the conflict-prone economy of a particular area.

Security and Business Environment

It is needless to say that business flourishes in a secure environment. Unpredictable socio-political environment directly affects investment decisions. Investors not only shy away from investing in new projects, they even withdraw funds from the existing projects as they are not sure about the returns that will be forthcoming from them and look for alternative opportunities elsewhere. The risk-averse business behaviour prompts the investors to keep new investment proposals on hold. Moreover, as the lending agencies hike the risk premiums, cost of borrowing funds goes up which necessitates higher returns from investments. As the lack of business confidence precludes such higher returns, lending becomes economically unviable. Thus, lack of investment in a conflict-prone economy negatively impacts on employment generation, income, and market demand. The role of the private sector in economic development is thus severely restricted. In such circumstances, higher public-sector expenditure is called for even in order to maintain the statuesque. This perhaps explains as to why in spite of substantial budgetary allocations, the economies of the northeastern states do not show any perceptible sign of progress.

Besides this negative impact of militancy on general business environment, the ethnic content of militant movements and business has further bearing on deteriorating economic condition in the NER. It may be pointed out that while the militant movements are rooted in the indigenous ethnic formations, business in the northeastern states is in the hands of the so-called ethnic 'others'. An anatomy of the entrepreneurial class that has historically evolved in the northeastern states indicates that wholesale business is controlled by the non-indigenous Marwaris, Punjabis, and Sindhis, while much of the retail trade is controlled by the non-indigenous Bengalis, Assamese, and Biharis. Although a class of nouveau riche has emerged in all the indigenous communities particularly through a politician–contractor–supplier nexus, emerging indigenous class often works only as commission agents in collaboration with the 'ethnic others'. The indigenous nouveau riche prefers to remain as 'sleeping partners' perhaps because of their lack of exposure to the value chain of the modern business.

The fact that while the members of indigenous ethnic groups organize militant movements seeking change of the political status of their respective homelands (whatever may be the degree of autonomy they ask for), the ethnic 'others' work for economic change (obviously in pursuit of profit). As the relationship between the 'host' and 'others' is often unfriendly if not hostile perhaps due to the fact that the mobilization of the members of the host community is often sought citing the 'others' as political or economic adversaries, ethnic identity of the 'others' itself, thus, becomes a source of insecurity. This is more so when the ethnic-militant movements, under the garb of ethno-national patriotism, seek to draw resources from the entrepreneurial 'others'.

Because of the fragile interethnic relationship between the host communities and entrepreneurial others, the foot soldiers of economic change find little incentives for shouldering the additional risks of business expansion. As militant movements sharpen the dividing lines between the indigenous and outsiders and often penalize the latter for doing business in the former's homeland by way of imposing protection taxes, the entrepreneurial class faces a hostile business environment that negatively influence their investment decisions.

Security and Flight of Capital

Deteriorating security environment encourages flight of capital in more than one ways. It is a herculean task to estimate the quantum of capital that flows away from a conflict-prone economy over time. As capital tends to migrate from areas having lesser opportunities to areas having higher opportunities, irrespective of security environment, it is difficult to classify the quantum of capital that has migrated due to hostile security environment and the quantum that has migrated elsewhere for better opportunities. However, as the militant movements create a feeling of insecurity in the business psyche, which, in turn, reduces business opportunities, there exists some sort of correspondence between these two. A significant amount of capital moves out of the region to buy consumer items which otherwise could have been produced within the region had there been normalcy. The militant movements act as disincentive for investment in productive activities as the entrepreneurs are targeted for rent seeking by the militant organizations. The larger the scale of business operation, the higher the rent one has to pay. As a result, there is a tendency on the part of the existing business at least not to grow outwardly. Instead of entering into productive activities, most business entities prefer to act as selling outlets. They procure goods from outside and sell them in the local markets. This form of business helps them to camouflage as small operators and invites less demand for rent from the militant organizations. Besides this, businesses in conflict-prone NER do not intend to acquire assets beyond the bare minimum so that they could relocate themselves or suspend their operations at short notice if such occasions arise. As productive activities require investment in fixed assets that contribute to fixed costs, frequent suspension of business activities that warrants from frequent calls for *bandhs*, strikes, road blockades, etc., do not make such acquisitions economically viable. As a result, economy remains essentially a consumer economy with a very weak linkage between the local resource base and production structure.

Besides consumption expenditure, migration of capital also takes place as the businesses in conflict-prone areas strive for developing alternative opportunities elsewhere so that in case of need they can fall back on them. In fact, accumulated capital from the NER finds its way to other parts of the country through intra-business route. Business diversification which could not be achieved in the NER due to security reasons is often carried out elsewhere. Thus, profit made by the businesses in the NER goes outside the region for investment.

Besides business, considerable amount of capital migrates from the NER to other regions through institutional routes. This is evident from the low credit-deposit ration of the scheduled commercial banks in the states of the NER shown in Table 4.1.

Table 4.1: Credit-deposit Ratio of Scheduled Commercial Banks in the Northeastern States (as on 31 March)

State	*1996*	*1998*	*2001*	*2002*	*2004*	*2005*	*2006*	*2007*	*2008**	*2009**	*2010**
Arunachal Pradesh	10.4	13.1	17.2	15.8	17.2	24.4	25.07	26.81	31.7	25.5	25.1
Assam	39.3	32.9	32.4	31.4	30.8	34.4	41.97	43.30	42.4	38.5	37.0
Manipur	53.7	58.8	39.0	25.4	29.1	41.0	50.66	53.40	48.4	36.0	40.6
Meghalaya	14.4	15.2	16.8	18.0	36.9	45.3	39.36	35.84	33.2	28.3	25.0
Mizoram	16.2	23.2	25.6	25.9	38.3	51.0	51.52	53.89	62.9	57.9	47.5
Nagaland	27.4	18.3	14.0	12.6	16.9	22.9	22.32	28.90	34.0	30.8	29.8
Tripura	42.1	34.0	23.0	22.3	25.4	29.7	31.63	33.98	36.1	30.7	29.2
All India	61.9	55.5	58.5	62.3	58.7	66.0	72.50	75.02	74.4	72.6	72.7

Source: NEC (2006).

Note: * denotes figures as per sanction.

It may be discerned from Table 4.1 that credit-deposit ratio is much lower in all the northeastern states compared to the national average. This highly disproportionate credit-deposit ratio in the northeastern states is due to both the demand and supply constraints. While on the one hand, lesser investment opportunities in a peripheral region generate less demand for investible fund, on the other, due to higher risk in doing business, bankers adopt extra-cautious approach in lending funds to business. The interplay of both the demand-side and supply-side factors choke the flow of capital into the local economy leading to out-migration of capital from the region at the cost of her own development.

An interesting point may be noted that while low credit-deposit ratio obviously indicates lower credit flow in the economy of the NER, higher flow does not necessarily mean creation of higher assets or larger investment in productive sectors. It has been learnt that relatively higher credit-deposit ratio in Manipur is linked with the system of determination of extortion amount from many small players by the insurgent groups. The extortion/donation amount is based on the net pay of the salaried segment of the population. This fact encourages the salaried groups to borrow from the banks for buying the durable consumer goods. As the repayment is made through Equal Monthly Instalment (EMI) which is deducted from the monthly salary, the quantum of net salary gets reduced and hence one has to pay less to the coffer of the insurgent groups. This hypothesis, however, needs to be verified. No studies have yet been undertaken to find the impact of the extortion demand on the consumer behaviour. As a result future studies on this aspect might be revealing for the stakeholders of market economy (Singh 2011).

Besides business and banking sector, another significant amount of capital also out-migrates from the NER in the form of transfer income. The politics of violence practiced by the militant organizations in the northeastern states has deteriorated the academic environment. As the academic institutions have been converted into the recruitment grounds by the militant organizations, parents do not feel it safe to send their wards into them and hence a sizeable segment of the student population from the conflict-prone zones of the NER migrate every year to other parts of the country particularly to places like Delhi, Bangalore, and Pune for acquiring formal education. As the parents want to keep their wards away from the war theatre, those who can support send their children out of the region. Safety of the child is, in fact, paramount in the minds of the parents. This causes a huge transfer of income from the region which is required for the up keep of the children.

Besides education, health care services are also very poor in the conflict-prone areas of the NER. People have to move out to other parts of the country for any serious health problems due to the non-existence of specialty medical services and out-migration of successful medical professionals. A substantial capital flows out of the region on this count as well which could have been retained had there been normalcy and security of the medical practitioners.

Insurgency, Rent Seeking, and Resource Drain

Insurgent groups in the NER mobilize resources in variety of ways. In some cases like in Nagaland, NSCN (I-M) imposes 'house tax' (Sahani 2001) on every dwelling unit. In most of the northeastern states, militant movements impose 'toll tax'[1] (Sahani 2001) on vehicles on all major routes that pass through the territory under their control. As there are more than one insurgent groups operating in a state, commercial vehicles have to pay 'toll tax' for more than once while passing through a particular route. In Nagaland, Manipur, and Assam, insurgent groups impose 'protection tax' on the businesses and commercial establishments.

In places like Nagaland, the tax-collection system devised by the Naga militant groups is so widespread that even small service providers like porters, rickshaw pullers, barbers are also not spared from the tax net. As the non-compliance of the extortion (tax) demand is met with immediate retaliation that employs instruments like physical punishment, quite notice, kidnapping, and in some cases shooting and killing,[2] the quantum of resource mobilization is much higher than any formal tax-collection system.

Unlike Nagaland and Manipur, insurgent groups in Assam prefer to target the corporate houses for extortion rather than targeting the small-income earners. As besides the flourishing tea, oil, and timber industries, Assam houses a number of other public- and private-sector industries as well as wholesale-trading enterprises that makes corporate sector a lucrative source of extortion. Since the resource-based industries are located in the interior far-flung areas, they are all vulnerable from security point of view. Insurgent groups encash this security vulnerability and demand a hefty sum as 'protection fee'. Das (2001) has reported an incident where a tea company paid Rs 13.5 million to the erstwhile BdSF (a Bodo ethnic-militant organization). He also reported of another tea company which had shown Rs 1 crore as unexplained expenditure on security (read pay-off to insurgent groups) in their audited balance sheet. Even Tata Tea, one of the subsidiaries of Tata group of industries, one of the leading industrial houses of India, is accused of extending clandestine logistic support to ULFA in 1997 by Assam police (*Business Standard* 1 October 1997). Assam Police has also alleged that Williamson Magor, a leading tea producer in the state, has also paid Rs 15 million to a militant organization in one delivery (Rediff on the Net n.d.). Needless to mention, these evidences show only the tip of the iceberg. During the heyday of the militancy in Assam while it received tacit support from the ruling elite (during AGP regime) and had penetrated in all the spheres of public administration, sense of insecurity engulfed the business which had to buy peace through transfer of a huge amount of resources. Dasgupta (2001) estimated that during 1990–7, ULFA raised about Rs 500 crore from the tea industry in Assam. It was learnt that during 1990s while ULFA used to collect taxes at the rate of 50 paisa per kilogram from the tea gardens in areas under their influence, NDFB used to collect annually Rs 1,500–3,000 per hectare of tea land. It is estimated that while the extortion amount in case of a proprietary garden amounted at Rs 25 lakh, the same for bigger company was Rs 1 crore during the 1990s (Gokhale 1998).

Besides extortion, a huge amount of public resource meant for various public-welfare schemes and projects is also diverted to the coffer of the insurgent groups through a politician–bureaucrat–business–insurgent group nexus. Sahani (2001) has cited a classic case of resource diversion from Public Distribution System (PDS) in Assam. PDS items like rice, wheat, salt, kerosene oil, etc., were found to have been directed to open-market sales, the price differential between PDS and open market multiplied by the quantity of an item used to generate the excess revenue that was being shared by militant groups and their business surrogates. Sahani estimates that this conversion from PDS to open-market price used to generate excess revenue in millions per month and much of which used to go to the coffer of ULFA. Sahani (2001) has also cited as to how millions of rural development fund was being siphoned in Assam through politician–bureaucrat–contractor–insurgent group nexus. Indeed, siphoning of rural development fund seems to be one of the causes for the existence of extreme economic duality between the rural and urban areas of the NER. As the contractors, firms, and officials executing rural development projects are vulnerable to security threats from the militant organizations, they prefer to develop some sort of symbiotic relationship with the militants rather than contesting them. The failure on the part of the state to provide adequate security to project sites and to create an environment of rule of law compels the project-implementing agencies and businesses to buy security against so-called donation (read extortion). In Nagaland, Manipur, some parts of Assam, and Arunachal Pradesh, the insurgent groups use the local contractors as their 'front' and much of the rural development projects are executed through them as this modus operandi puts all the players including the politicians, bureaucrats, contractors, and insurgent in a win-win situation. All these players reap their dividends at the cost of the development projects and schemes meant for the welfare of the common people. Needless to mention, the central government is also aware of this political economy of diversion of public resource in the NER. Das (2001) has reported that the union rural development minister, in a meeting with his counterparts from the northeastern states at Shillong on 14 June 2001, has threatened to stop funding if the funds go to the coffer of the militant organizations.

A huge amount of fund collected annually by the insurgent groups through their system of taxation and other means regularly goes to buy arms from abroad particularly from the Southeast Asia markets as has already been hinted in Chapter 3. A significant portion of the fund of the militant groups also goes out of the region to maintain their organizational bases elsewhere. It has been reported that while NSCN (I-M) has developed considerable amount of commercial interest in Bankok,[3] capital of Thailand, ULFA has done the same in Dhaka, capital of Bangladesh (Kumar n.d.). ULFA and other northeast militant groups like HNLC and Achik National Volunteer Council (ANVC) are reported to have made significant investments in businesses like hotels and restaurants, healthcare, transport and plantations (Nag 2008).

Besides neighbouring countries of Bangladesh, Myanmar, and Nepal, some of the insurgent groups even have well-established bases overseas. It is difficult to guess as to how much money flows out on this count.[4] Since the lion's share of the fund mobilized by the insurgent groups flows out of the region, they are persistently bleeding the local economy into white (Das 2002a).

Insurgency, Drug Trade, and Social Cost

Resource mobilization efforts by the militant organizations often produce pernicious social effects. The best example is the involvement of the militant groups in narcotics trade. As Myanmar produces 80 per cent of heroine in the world, and many of the ethnic war groups like the Kachins, Karens, Mons, Shans, Chins, Kayah, Rakhine, and Wa in Myanmar have skilfully integrated insurgency with drug production and trade (Lintner 1994), ethnic insurgent groups of the NER in general and Manipur in particular, having liaison with their counterparts across the border, have also access to the drug-trade channels. In fact, Kuki National Army (KNA), which controls the Indo-Myanmar border trade route through the Moreh–Tamu sector, is known to control the drug-trafficking business between Myanmar and Manipur. Besides KNA, a number of Manipur-based militant groups play the feeder role within the Golden Triangle drug trail. The association between militancy and drug trade became evident when the UNLF cadres including its chairman Meghen were captured and jailed in Burma in 2001 for drug trafficking (Egreteau 2006). Further, Assam police had seized 27,000 capsules of spasmo proxyvon, a potent analgesic, used by intravenous drug users, from the activists of People's United Liberation Front (PULF), a Manipur-based militant group, in Guwahati in April 2008 (Hussain 2008). As they play the role of the career, the spill-over effects are felt in Manipur. Youth are easily taken to drugs due to its easy availability in the surroundings.

The easy availability of drugs in a fragile social, political, and economic environment has encouraged the frustrated youth to use them as sedative. This has a pernicious effect on the public health in the state. From 1986 till October 2007, out of 156,490 blood samples that were screened, 22,053 were reported HIV positive giving a sero-positivity rate of 14.09 per cent. This shows that out of every 100 sample 14 are reported HIV positive. Again of the total sample, 4,154 cases of AIDS had been reported indicating a rate of 2.65 per cent. In fact Manipur has the highest HIV prevalence in all the states in India. One can imagine the gravity of the situation given the state's high literacy rate and low per capita income (Singh 2011). This AIDS epidemic that grew out of consumption of drugs poses an enormous challenge before the state and society. A large part of family income and public health-care budget flows to address this menace which could have otherwise been used for productive purposes.

Insurgency, Corruption, and Cost of Doing Business

Insurgency helps in legitimizing corruption in public life. As the main source of resource mobilization by the insurgent groups is the diversion of public fund earmarked for various development activities as well as so-called 'professional tax' on the salaried group of people, 'protection tax' on the business, and 'beneficiary tax' on the contractors and suppliers, this diversion requires involvement of bureaucrats, government employees, businesses, suppliers, and contractors on the ground. People who pay these taxes and collaborate in the diversion of public funds do not do so without any premium. Rather, wherever possible, they use this to legitimize their efforts to seek rent from the services they render to others. Since the militant groups stand solidly behind these people, they get emboldened in their rent seeking pursuits and thereby spread the menace of corruption to permeate every sphere of public life.

Besides profitable ventures like government supply and construction works, even the basic services like permission for house construction by the civic bodies, house water and electricity connections, issue of driving licences, issue of birth certificates to new born babies, availing medical benefits by the government employees, appointment in any kind of government services, availing post retirement benefits, issue of caste certificate, purchase of any property that requires legal papers, etc., are all priced. In fact, the menace of corruption is so widespread that people often euphemistically call 'Manipur' as 'Money-pur' (*pur* for place, indicating that Manipur is a place where one can make easy money). Except Tripura and Meghalaya, the spirit of 'Money-pur' appears to be equally applicable for other northeastern states as well. The insurgent groups are benefitted by supporting corruption in several ways. First, they place higher extortion demands on the corrupt officials and mobilize higher amount of resources. Second, corruption acts as an instrument for diversion of public fund to the coffer of the insurgent groups. Third, corrupt officials are used as 'moles' for gathering information about the targets. Fourth, a degenerated and demoralized administration cannot fight against militancy effectively. Fifth, corruption eats away the legitimacy of governance and increases frustration in the psyche of the people. This may encourage the youth to join militancy.

What is more important is the negative impact of corruption on economic development. As economic development in northeastern states is largely state-engineered rather than market-guided, the prevalence of widespread corruption in public life has a severe crippling effect on local economic development. Firstly, corruption yields low-quality public works. As a significant part of the fund earmarked for the public projects is siphoned off, the life of the projects gets reduced. This increases the cost of maintenance of the existing projects manifold and hence reduces the chance of taking up new projects. Thus, while existing projects are used as 'golden geese', which generate huge unaccounted income as the same old work is cited as new for a number of times, new projects are hardly undertaken for paucity of fund. As a result, infrastructure, the sine qua non for economic development, has remained extremely weak in most of the northeastern states.

It may be pointed out that the nature of corruption that usually takes place in the peripheral and fragile states of the NER does not fully corroborate the way the issue of corruption is addressed in an competitive-market environment. In economic literature, corruption is often viewed as 'speed money' particularly when government machinery follows cumbersome procedures for granting, say permits or licences. In such cases, 'corruption is the much-needed grease for the squeaking wheels of a rigid administration' (Bardhan 1997). It is even often argued that in a competitive situation, corruption may lead to allocation efficiency as the lowest cost firms can only be the 'highest bidder in bribes' (Bardhan 1997). However, there is no denying of the fact that corruption adversely affects the growth process in an economy. 'A payment of bribes to get an investment license clearly reduces the incentive to invest' (Bardhan 1997).

In case of the NER, corruption is prominent particularly in public expenditure by the subunit governments. Public resources meant for 'productivity-enhancing infrastructure', to use Bardhan's phraseology, public-utility services, and poverty-alleviation programmes are diverted for the private benefits of the politicians, bureaucrats, contractors, and suppliers as well as, in some cases, for the benefits of the militant groups. As a result economic growth and public welfare are certain to decline. It is extremely difficult for the private sector to grow in an environment of low economic growth and high rent seeking. As return to entrepreneurship declines in a slow-growing economy relative to those to rent seeking, a rise in rent seeking activities (may be due to the growth in number of the rent seekers) will further slow down growth. Although historical evidences suggest that corruption declines with the economic growth as 'prospering economy can also afford to pay its civil servants well' (Bardhan 1997), the experience of the northeastern states suggests that the otherwise also seems to hold good. In them, low economic growth is accompanied with high level of corruption which has reduced return on investment. This is acting as a disincentive for the growth of the private sector which is extremely important for the creation of jobs and incomes particularly for the educated unemployed youth who are the driving force behind the thriving militancy in the region. In the absence of the growth of the private sector, economic underdevelopment keeps on perpetuating. Thus, corruption is one of the important triggers for the vicious cycle of low growth, unemployment, and militancy in the NER. As far as the NER is concerned, instead of 'greasing', corruption is 'sanding the wheels' (Aidt 2009).

It may also be noted that while the focus of much of the literature on corruption is to assess its growth-enhancing or growth-reducing impacts, the socio-political and psychological impacts are not generally taken into consideration. Corruption eats away the legitimacy of governance of a regime, adds to the frustration, and encourages people to rebel against the government. The rebel groups use the corrupt images of the power elite and cash on the anti-establishment sentiments of the people in their recruitment strategy. Thus, corruption often aggravates conflict. There is no dearth of instances where corruption has added to the fragility of a state. The *World Development Report* (World Bank 2011) refers the case of rebellion in Liberia in 1980 where government corruption had been the prime motivator. Erosion of legitimacy that invites peoples' backlash and political instability in a way is more harmful than loss in GDP/Gross State Domestic Product (GSDP) due to corruption.

Why is it that northeastern states tend to be more corrupt than many of the mainland states in India? Except Tripura and Meghalaya, all other five states in the region, namely, Arunachal Pradesh, Assam, Manipur, Mizoram, and Nagaland appear to be highly corrupt. Although there is no systematic and holistic corruption perception study on the Indian states, Transparency International India and Centre for Media Studies (CMS) together have conducted a few limited corruption perception studies. Their Indian Corruption Study 2005 involving eleven public services and twenty major Indian states places Assam as one of the highly corrupt states, sixth from the bottom. However, except Assam, none of the other northeastern states is included in this study.

There are three main factors for high-corruption level in the NER. First, as the region lies in the Indian periphery, it is also out of focus from national media. The physical and emotional isolation of the region provides the necessary shield to the local power elite whose corruption activities go unnoticed. Second, the weak emotional bonding of the people of the NER with the mainstream politics and culture does not allow the national political parties to penetrate the grassroots, the regional political elite take this advantage and practice a system of patronage rather than a system of performance in order to mobilize their vote banks. Expediency of electoral interests dictates the power elite to accommodate the interests of the militant groups in siphoning public resources for private gains. Third, existence of weak institutional structures and non-transparency in public policy enable the power elite to divert public funds for private gratification.

How do we, then, explain the cases of Meghalaya and Tripura where the menace of corruption in public offices appears to be low? The plausible explanation for Meghalaya seems to lie with its unique federal arrangement. The three major constituents of Meghalaya polity, namely the Khasis, the Garos, and the Jaintias, have their own ADC created under the Sixth Schedule of the Indian constitution. The devolution of power and finance among these ADCs and decentralization of public initiatives appear to have been acting as a mechanism of check and balance. Unlike a centralized system of governance, striking corrupt deals in a decentralized system which requires the formation of cartels among the power elite and bureaucrats at different levels is not easy. My hunch is that it is this decentralized governance structure that has made a difference in case of Meghalaya.

As far as Tripura is concerned, there is a positive shift from more corrupt to less corrupt practices in governance. Before the Left Front government came to power in 1993, the corruption perception of Tripura was as good as any other high corrupt Indian state. In fact good governance and transparent public life of the local leaders have made a difference.

Insurgency, Non-development Expenditure, and Distorted Goals

In a situation of strife, political expediency becomes the cardinal principle for resource allocation rather than economic efficiency. The state apparatus is geared up to achieve political goals, namely, political stability, legitimacy of particular regime, and establishment of authority of the state. In achieving these, immediate results get precedence over the ultimate cause of people's welfare. Privileges are showered upon those sections and groups who play significant role in shaping public opinions and who legitimize the rule of the regime. Thus, priorities are not ordered on the basis of the maxims of rationality of market economics. Rather they are determined by the interest of the power elite in terms of their creation and holding the support bases. This leads to wasteful and unproductive expenditure in all the northeastern states.

As the horizontal inequality is one of the major drivers for the growth of militancy in the NER, one group's demand for homeland and state privileges often conflicts with the interest of another. As a result, they often engage in internecine warfare. The region has experienced a number of violent interethnic riot, genocide, and massacre. For example, Tripuri–Bengali conflict in Tripura in 1980 (the Mandai Massacre), Assamese–Muslim Bengali conflict in Assam in February 1983 (the Nellie Massacre), Kuki–Naga conflict in Manipur during 1992–4, Arunachalee–Chakma conflict in Arunachal Pradesh in 1994, Mizo–Reang conflict in Mizoram in 1997, Karbi–Dimasa conflict in Assam in October 2005, Bodo–Santhal conflict in Assam in December 2005, and Khasi–Karbi conflict in Meghalaya in October 2005. Each of these conflicts resulted into deaths, destitutions, and human sufferings. In case of the Nellie Massacre, according to official estimates, 2,191 people were killed (unofficial claims put the figure at more than 5,000),[5] and several thousands were displaced. Like the Nellie Massacre, all other interethnic conflicts have resulted into large-scale violence, deaths, and displacement. All these require a stupendous humanitarian assistance.

Besides compensations to the families of the deceased, huge fund is required to maintain the IDPs in camps and their subsequent rehabilitation. The affected people require a considerable time to engage themselves in gainful activities. The diversion of funds from productive to humanitarian upkeep activities no doubt adversely affects the growth process of the state concerned. Moreover, conflict in one northeastern state puts the burden of Internally Displaced Persons (IDP) on the other. The spill-over effects of an ethnic conflict across the boundary not only cripples the growth process of the neighbouring states but also generates ethnic tensions that threaten their political stability.

Governance in a conflict-ridden environment involves higher administrative expenditure particularly for meeting both routine and emergency security expenses. As the security expenses are not subject to routine audit surveillance, enough room is left for misuse of public fund under this head. Diversion of development fund for such unforeseen security needs has been a common phenomenon in northeastern states. This tendency towards misappropriation of public fund in the name of security exigencies meets with little resistance due to the non-functioning of the social and political institutions at different levels of the governance structure of the conflict-ridden societies.

What is more important is the fact that occurrence of repeated violence changes the development focus of the local governments. As people at large prefer a peaceful environment, the power elite assume the role of the peace broker rather than delivering the public goods. Their failure to deliver public goods which people value in life is conveniently shifted to the entrepreneurs of violence. The thesis of trade-off between development and violence is meticulously sold to people to justify the incompetencies of the power elite and their new-found role as peace builders. For electoral gains, the power elite often in collision with the security manager's stage, manage surrender of certain militants only to hoodwink the peace-loving electorate. Thus, in conflict situations, the agenda of governance gets transformed from development to restoration of peace. Elections are fought not against the parameters of development but for the ability of conflict management. Thus, the idea of development gets distorted with the repeated occurrence of violence.

Insurgency, Human Security, and Development

Right to life, livelihood, and security are the most basic elements of human security that are linked to human development (UNDP 2005). Human development is the process of widening choices for people to do and be what they value in life. These choices are widened while social, political, and economic opportunities are expanded (UNDP 2004). In a number of ways, like any other conflict-ridden areas, insurgency, violence, and recurring conflict are adversely affecting human security and development in the NER. Although no systematic and undisputed account of human casualties arising out of civil wars conducted by various ethno-militant groups is available, one estimate suggests that since 1947, at least 50,000 people were killed in the NER (IDMC 2006). At least 10,000 people have been killed in Assam in between 1980 and 2005 (IDMC 2006) indicating 400 deaths in a year and more than 1 death a day during this period. Singh (2011) has reported that between 1992 and 2008, there were 4,857 insurgency-related killings in Manipur indicating 304 deaths every year, 25 per month, 6 per week, and 1 death in every 29 hours. Similarly, more than 4,000 people were killed in Tripura between 1980 and 2004 (IDMC 2006) indicating 167 deaths per year, 14 per month,

month, and almost one killing in every alternate day. Indeed, Assam, Manipur, and Tripura had been the killing fields where state had failed miserably to protect the human life.

Besides killing, the NER has been one of the hotspots for conflict-related IDP in Asia. Although no credible data is available on the IDPs, each state in the NER has a history of waves of violence which have uprooted thousands of people and disrupted their pattern of livelihood. The ethnic cleansing of the Santhals by the Bodos in Assam in 2005 had displaced an estimated 250,000 persons (IDMC 2006). In Karbi–Dimasa conflict, about 50,000 people were displaced and hundreds lost their lives. Tripuri–Bengali conflict in Tripura in 1980 had killed 1,300 persons, displaced 189,919 persons, 34,661 houses were gutted and loss of property was estimated at about Rs 21 crore (Chakravarti 2002). The Mizo–Reang conflict in Mizoram in 1997 had sent 37,000 IDPs in Tripura (Debbarma 2002). The Kuki–Naga conflict in Manipur in 1992 had killed more than 1,000 persons, and displaced 130,000 persons (IDMC 2006), 600 villages had been uprooted, and more than 10,000 houses belonging to both the communities had been torched (Haokip 2002). These incidents of violence and consequent death and displacement figures are cited only by way of examples. A systematic spatio-temporal study can only reveal the colossal dimensions of violation of human security caused due to recurrence of interethnic violence in the NER.

Both deaths and collapse of livelihood due to displacement have long-term adverse effects on the welfare of the victim population as well as people residing in their neighbourhood. As the men participate actively in violence, their death not only puts their families in duress but also causes loss of the bread earners, making their dependents destitute. Disruption of livelihood breaks the production, income, consumption patterns as well as educational and health-related support systems of the families. Children become the worst sufferers.

Education and health, the two most important determinants of human development, are severely affected by recurrence of violence, displacement, and deterioration of internal security condition. Educational and health institutions are often burned as they symbolize the public property situated in remote areas. These are also used to house the displaced people in case of any eventualities. In an insecure environment, parents also discourage the children particularly the girls to attend regular classes. As children are soft targets for recruitment in militant groups, they are often kidnapped by the militant groups; this acts as a disincentive for the parents to send their wards to school. In 2008, a number of child-kidnapping cases have been reported in Manipur. Media report confirms that 45 children have been kidnapped supposedly by the two armed militant groups of Manipur namely People's Revolutionary Party of Kangleipak (PREPAK) and PREPAK Cobra Task Force in order to recruit them as child soldiers (Thakuria 2008).

Recruitment of child soldiers is rampant in many of the conflict-ridden societies particularly in Africa like Sudan and Somalia. It is understood that nearly 300,000 children in approximately seventeen countries around the globe are being forced to participate in the war. These children, who have been denied a childhood and even subjected to horrific violence, serve as soldiers for both the government and rebel groups. Equipped with sophisticated arms, these soldiers work as carriers (of messages and supplies to the conflict zones) and also as human mine detectors. Many times, they are used as suicide bombers (Thakuria 2008). Devoid of education, family care, and social values, these children become the torch bearer of the terror machine in later life. The return on training in violence is further violence.

Interethnic violence drastically reduces the mobility of the ordinary people particularly across the cross-cultural social spaces. Polarization along ethnic lines creates 'identity boxes', to use Sen's (2006b) phraseology, and people of one community feel insecure to move into the areas inhabited by other community. A Meitei school teacher in Manipur employed in a school located in the Naga inhabited area fears to go to the school for perceived insecurity. A Bengali doctor in Tripura posted in a health centre located in tribal inhabited area could hardly attend to his duties during the heyday of interethnic conflicts. As the state could not ensure the security of the service provider, it can not force the person or agencies to perform. As a result, both the educational and health-care systems in conflict-prone areas have become dysfunctional. As a result, violence has removed the 'ladder', to use Chang's (2002) terminology, using which the poor could have broken the vicious cycle of poverty.

Freedom is one of the important determinants of human development (Sen 2006a). Violence curbs freedom of the citizens in a number of ways. In a conflict-ridden society political space often gets polarized between the state and non-state militant forces leaving hardly any space for civil society. In an open environment, public-policy debates, criticisms and suggestions play an important role in choosing the best among the alternative public actions. All public offices, institutions, and organizations work under public scrutiny. Media, print or electronic, plays a vital role by providing a domain for public debates. Once a society enters into a conflict trap, this public domain gets squeezed. Decisions and actions of the authoritative militant organizations are imposed on the society on gunpoint. As the militant leaders are not under electoral compulsion, they do not have any accountability to the people for whom they ostensibly wage the war. As a war strategy, both the state and the militant groups compete to control the media. While the state uses its legal power to control and mould the media in its favour, the militant groups flex their muscle for the same. In Manipur, the militant groups use threat to the lives of the reporters, editors, and outright forceful ban of the publication or broadcasting in order to tame the media (Singh 2011). In Nagaland, people can hardly participate in public debate about the fight of the Naga groups against the Indian state. As the militant groups hardly respect any human rights, they just eliminate their critics. Intense feeling of insecurity has engulfed the conflict-ridden societies where people fear to express their opinion on the matters relating to their welfare—economic, business, political, or social issues.

Interethnic conflict and violence also adversely affect human development by way of drastically curtailing the cultural liberty of the citizens. As the social, political, and economic opportunities do not guarantee cultural liberty which is viewed as one of the central aspects of human development, states must actively promote the practice of multiculturalism by its citizens. In fact, 'cultural liberty is about allowing people the freedom to choose their identities—and to lead the lives they value—without being excluded from other choices important to them' (UNDP 2004). Ethnic militancy primarily rooted in politics of identity poses a tremendous challenge in fostering cultural liberty in the societies of the NER. The irredentist ideology of the Naga,

Bodo, Karbi, Dimasa, Kuki, Tripuri, and Meitei insurgent groups has led to intense interethnic feeling of distrust and hatred. Many of these groups at one point in time or other have engaged in ethnic cleansing killing thousands of people belonging to other groups as has been mentioned earlier. This has transformed the social spaces in the northeastern states from multiculturalism to plural monoculturalism (Das 2008b). In Manipur, insurgent groups have banned the screening of Hindi movies since 1990s, imposed traditional dress code for the women, and fanned up public emotion for the change of Meitei script from Bengali to Meitei Mayek (traditional Meitei script used about 300 years before) (Singh 2011). Other militant groups in the NER also prefer people to stick to tradition and orthodoxy that are perceived to better protect their identity without understanding the value of infusion of cultural diversities in human development.

Social capital, which is found to have played an important role in sustainable development of a society, is also adversely affected by interethnic conflict and violence. Social capital refers to the institutions, relationships, and norms that shape the quality and quantity of a society's social interactions (World Bank 1998). Growth of militancy and violence in the NER has undermined both the traditional and non-traditional social institutions. As the social institutions provide a stable framework in which human interaction take place (North 1990), undermining their authority without any alternative institutional structure has created a void. While, on the one hand, the collapse of community authority structure, interpersonal trust deficit, decline in legitimacy, shattering of interethnic relationships, and breakdown of both vertical and horizontal social networks have eroded the 'Putnam effects' (associations facilitate growth by increasing trust), and, on the other, the penetration of the militant organizations into the institutional and organizational structures and their growing links with similar groups within and across the border has strengthened the 'Olson effects' (associations stifle growth through rent seeking) to the detriment of the society.

Ethnic militancy, by triggering the interethnic conflict and violence, also widens the horizontal inequality which in turn triggers further conflict and violence. The communities living in far-flung areas from the major urban areas which act as centres of production and distribution of goods and services suffer more having unequal access to markets and public goods than the communities living in those centres. Communities in remote areas also feel more insecure than their counterparts in urban areas which serve as the headquarters of administration and security forces. Smaller communities having lesser bargaining powers in a number-based democracy could hardly access the state privileges. As the development projects in a multiethnic society are likely to be located in areas inhabited by the majority community, horizontal inequality widens among the minorities which adds further fragility to interethnic relations. The politics of identity practiced by the ethno-national movements and their militant wings thus pushes a multiethnic society towards a conflict trap.

Insurgency, Subversive Activities, and Economic Development

Subversive activities of the insurgent groups not only add to human penury by way of loss of lives, disruption of livelihood, and displacement but also reduce the stock of physical capital in a conflict-ridden society. The destruction of oil pipelines and other infrastructure of the oil industry by ULFA in Assam, destruction of electricity transformers and communication towers by the militant groups in Manipur, destruction of railway tracks and bridges by Bodo militant groups in Assam are some examples which adversely affect the existing stock of physical capital that warrants a huge public investment for their replacement. Destruction of physical capital not only involves the additional cost for their replacement, it also entails the loss of income that could have been accrued to the society as well as stream of future income that could have been generated had the same investment been made for the procurement of new assets. By destroying the past investment, choking the present income stream, and stopping the future flow of investment, recurrent violence reverses the growth momentum in an economy. On the basis of growth baselines for cross-country panel data for last 50 years, researchers have estimated the costs of civil wars to range from 1.6–2.3 percentage of GDP per year of violence (UNDP 2011). However, this inverse growth-conflict relationship can not be ascertained in the northeastern states primarily due to the federal transfer of resources from the centre to the states.

Nonetheless, if one looks into the ratio of central grant and state's own resources in the annual revenue accounts of the northeastern states, one can find that either the share of state's own resources is stagnant or declining as percentage of total annual revenue receipts in all the conflict-ridden states in the NER which indirectly proves the inverse growth-conflict hypothesis. Take for instance the case of Assam, which is relatively developed of all the northeastern states, the Comptroller and Auditor General (CAG) report (2007) shows that share of state's revenue had remained stagnant at 39 per cent for consecutive five years during the 2002/3–2006/7. Similarly in Manipur, the state's share of resources was 9 per cent during 2004–5, 7 per cent during 2005–6, 11 per cent during 2006–7, again 9 per cent during 2007–8, and 11 per cent during 2008–9 (CAG 2009). This shows very poor performance of the state. Out of every Rs 100 spent by the Manipur government during 2008–9, only Rs 11 had been contributed by the people of the state and the rest came from the centre by way of state's share of union taxes and grants in aid. Due to depressed business environment, the state's share of union taxes does not constitute any significant amount. On an average the grants in aid constituted more than 75 per cent of the state's total revenue during 2004–9 in Manipur indicating heavy dependence of the state on the centre.

Besides destroying the past investment, recurrent violence by the militant groups in the NER has also escalated the cost of the present development projects manifold. The frequent attack on the project sites, kidnapping of project engineers, killing of project workers, destroying of project goods by the Dimasa militant groups in North Cachar Hills have caused an inordinate delay in the implementation of railway–gauge conversion between Lumding and Silchar in Assam as well as stalled the progress of the work on East–West Road corridor connecting Silchar (Assam) with Porbandar (Gujarat). Both the projects will benefit the people of North Cachar Hills, South Assam, Manipur, Mizoram, and Tripura who are suffering from lack of connectivity for long. Besides the loss in social welfare, the cost escalation due to time overrun for both the projects is enormous.

Recurrent violence, by raising the risk factor, acts as disincentive for the flow of future investment. In spite of being rich in natural resources, the region could neither attract the domestic private investment nor FDI.

Apart from location factor, insecurity further adds to the disincentive. Although India is experiencing a significant rise in the inflow of FDI that has energized growth in different regions, it has bypassed the NER as the region has received only 0.1 per cent of the cumulative flow of FDI in the country during 2000–10 (DPIP 2010).

Insurgency and State Fragility Syndrome

The politics of identity, ethno-national movements, ethnic militancy, and interethnic conflicts have created a socio-political environment in the NER where neither the citizens nor the communities feel secure. The tacit alignment of the state with the interest of the dominant community in a multiethnic society has eroded its legitimacy to the minority communities. It may be mentioned that the states in the NER have failed to deliver justice and remove the apprehensions in the minds of the members of the minority communities that their interests would be protected under law. Nobody was punished for the Nellie Massacre that took thousands of lives of the minority Muslim community in Assam in 1983. As part of the investigation, 688 criminal cases were filed in and of these 310 cases were chargesheeted. The remaining 378 cases were closed due to the police claim of 'lack of evidence'. But all the 310 chargesheeted cases were dropped by the AGP government as a part of Assam Accord. As a result not a single person has even had to face trial for the gruesome massacre. A Commission of Inquiry was instituted under Tribhubhan Prasad Tiwary, the report of which has not been made public.[6] Similar is the experience in other genocides where thousands of people were killed in Kuki–Naga conflict in Manipur, Tripuri–Bengali conflict in Tripura, Bodo–Santhals conflict, and Karbi–Dimasa conflict in Assam. In all these cases, the northeastern states not only failed to protect the citizens' right to life, provide adequate relief to the victims, arrange their rehabilitation but also failed to deliver justice. The failure of the states compelled the members to bank on their respective ethnic-militant groups for security and justice.

The identity politics of AASU, AGP, and AXX combined in Assam during the 1970s and 1980s has encouraged other ethnic groups in the state to organize and intensify ethno-national movements in order to protect their respective community interests. The irredentist ideology of the Naga movement for cessation has led to formation of a number of Kuki militant groups in the hills of Manipur. During the Naga–Kuki conflict, each community was looking at their respective ethno-militant groups for security and justice as the state had completely failed to protect the lives of the members of both the communities. In fact, eighteen Kuki militant groups have sprung up in Manipur and Mizoram at different points in time and majority of whom are now under ceasefire agreement. Similarly, Bodo–Santhal conflict has led to the mushrooming of Adhivasi militant groups in Assam as the state has utterly failed to protect the lives of the Santhal who have been instrumental in creating huge wealth by way of working in the tea gardens in Assam for centuries. Immediately after the conflict, All Adhivasi National Liberation Army was formed in 2006 to protect the interests of the Adhivasi community in Assam. Some of the old and decaying Adhivasi militant organizations like Adhivasi Cobra Force (formed in mid-1990s), Adhivasi Cobra Militant Force (formed in 1996), Birsa Commando Force (formed in 1997) got a new lease of life. Several other groups have come up overnight. All these indicate that the state has lost its legitimacy among the warring communities and the monopoly of the state for using coercion is seriously challenged by the ethno-militant groups in the region. The lack of good governance, failure to provide public goods, poor capacity to promote development, and weak authority of the northeastern states has created an environment that resembles the symptoms of state fragility (Brecher and Wilkenfeld 1990; Carment *et al.* 2010; Gurr 1970).

Having discussed the economic cost of insurgency by way of severe erosion of all forms of capital—physical, working, social, and human—and creation of an environment of state fragility, we may now turn to the other side of the conflict-development discourse, that is, how lack of economic development can exacerbate conflict? Or how development can help in the prevention or resolution of conflict? Is there any direct relationship between economic underdevelopment and violence? If not, how these two are interlinked?

Economic Underdevelopment and Violence

Underdeveloped economic base acts as a driver of conflict in more than one ways particularly in a multiethnic society where the degree of access to public resources is different for the different communities. This differential access may be due to historically evolved pattern of privileges among different communities or due to differential positions in state power and authority or due to differential electoral strength in a number-based democracy. In low-growth environment, unequal distribution hardly leaves anything for the marginalized groups resulting into intense feeling of relative deprivation and the demand for political cessation. In a low-growth environment, the capacity of the state to provide public goods remains weak compared to their demand which may lead to violent manifestations. Economic underdevelopment is associated with less livelihood opportunities for the growing population resulting into a large-scale unemployment and underemployment which in turn may fuel rebellion.

Collier (2007) observed a link between risk of civil war and low level of income. He estimated that a typical low-income country faces a risk of civil war of about 14 per cent in any five-year period. A rise in growth rate by one percentage point reduces the risk by one percentage point. Collier (2007) feels that low-income and low-growth environment is associated with poverty and hopelessness which drive the youth to join rebel group in search of 'a small chance of riches'. Also, United Nations Development Programme (UNDP 2011) has noted that low incomes reduce the opportunity cost of engaging in violence. As the marginal cost of rebellion is negligible, it pays to rebel in low-income countries. Since people have little to lose in waging war, risk of civil war is more in a low-growth economic environment (Tschirgi *et al.* 2010). These factors have led to the establishment of strong statistical correlation between low levels of GDP per capita and the risk of conflict (Tschirgi *et al.* 2010).

Most of the conflict-ridden countries in the world are poor. Somalia, Rwanda, Democratic Republic of Congo, Uganda, Cote d'Ivoire, Afghanistan, Angola, Colombia, Liberia, Sierra Leone, and Sudan are all trapped in low growth and poverty.

In fact low-income countries suffer from all the three gaps— security gaps, capacity gaps, and legitimacy gaps—extremely vital for sustainable development and good governance (UNDP 2004). Low-income does not allow a state to protect the human security including the right to livelihood as they lack in economic opportunities for their citizens to enjoy a decent life. The higher social, economic, and environmental risks in such countries intensify the risk of violence. The capacity gaps arise out of the failure of the governments to provide public goods and social welfare services that people value in their life. The legitimacy gaps arise either due to dysfunctional nature of institutional structure that could hardly mediate the inter-group conflict of interests. However, economic underdevelopment may not be the direct cause of conflict, but it creates a socio-economic environment conducive for violence to thrive.

In case of the NER, identity and autonomy movements of the Nagas, Mizos, ethnic Assamese, Bodos, Karbis, Dimasas, Tripuris, Meiteis, Hmars, and Kukis assumed altogether different dimensions due to the underdeveloped economic base in which these ethnic groups live. Lack of economic opportunities poses a powerful threat to the survival of these communities. The ethno-national movements not only sought political and cultural autonomy to protect their ethnic identity but also a space to monopolize the economic opportunities.

The lower opportunity cost for engaging in violence has swelled the cadre strengths and support bases of these movements. Although econometric studies have failed to find any correlation between unemployment and violence (UNDP 2011), case studies, on the contrary have suggested a strong association between them. Menkhaus (2010) has analyzed the role of 'youth bulge' hypothesis in making Somalia a heaven for civil war. With very low literacy rate among the young adults, fuelling problems of unemployment in Somalia encourages youth to join the militant groups that, in turn, raise the level of social violence. Akiner (2010) has described the link between unemployment and social violence in Tajikistan. In post-Soviet Tajikistan, Tajik youth from rural areas migrated in the cities in a large number but failed to integrate themselves with the urban ethos and culture. They remained in the margin of the urban society and were easily drawn into gun and drug culture. The process has led to the development of a youth subculture that was characterized by alienation, frustration, and pent-up aggression (Akiner 2010).

As far as the northeastern states are concerned, agriculture is the predominant livelihood of the majority of the people. As per the 2001 Census data, cultivators and agricultural labourers together constitute 61.7 per cent of the workers in Arunachal Pradesh. The same for

Assam, Manipur, Meghalaya, Mizoram, Nagaland, and Tripura is 52.3, 52.2, 65.8, 60.6, 68.3, and 50.8 per cent, respectively (Census of India 2001). Given the very weak industrial base in all the northeastern states, the size of disguised unemployment in agriculture appears to be quite high. High literacy rate in most of the northeastern states along with weak economic structure has given birth to a significant quantum of educated unemployment. The educated unemployment problem has become the greatest challenge for all the governments in the northeastern states particularly for Assam and Manipur. A study of the employment exchange data of Manipur for the period 1981/82–2002/03 (Das and Singh 2007) shows that the average annual growth of registrants on the live register stands at 13,718 persons whereas the average annual placement for the same period comes around 464 persons. This implies that it takes twenty-nine years, assuming the average annual rate of placement for the period continues in future, to absorb the additional job seekers that appear in the job market in one year. This indicates the horrible unemployment situation, that is, prevailing in Manipur.

The implication of this large-scale educated unemployment for the growth of militancy in Manipur is captured by the case studies. Kshetri (2006) took a sample of 100 surrendered militants in order to find the unemployment–insurgency linkage in Manipur. The distribution of these hundred militants by educational qualifications shows that only one person was illiterate, one had primary education, thirty-three had high school-level education, thirty were matriculate, twenty-two were undergraduate, twelve were graduate, and one was postgraduate. Of them, ninety-seven reported to be unemployed before they had joined the rebel groups. Furthermore, 84 per cent of the respondents had come from the low-income groups.

In a similar study, Singh (2010) took fifty surrendered militants in Manipur to examine the unemployment–insurgency linkages. In his sample, six were below matriculate, thirty-four were matriculate, thirty-six undergraduates, twenty-two graduates, and two persons were classified as having 'other' categories of qualification which Singh did not specify. Out of the fifty, forty respondents, that is, 80 per cent, have reported to be unemployed before joining the militant groups. Another 10 per cent have reported to have been working as farmers.

Forty-four respondents, that is, 88 per cent of the total, were found to have come from low-income groups.

It is, thus, evident from these case studies that low-income base as well as high educated unemployment acts as powerful motivation for the youth to join militancy. Given the underdeveloped nature of the economies of the northeastern states characterized by traditional agriculture, very weak industrial base and over-saturated-government-sector-centred tertiary activities, like Manipur, unemployment and low-income conditions drive the youth in other northeastern states as well to join the militancy. In most cases, unemployment–insurgency linkages in the NER work through social identity dynamics rather than purely cost-benefit motives. This fact rules out the possibility of establishing any direct quantitative relationship between unemployment and violence.

In Assam the identity crisis of the ethnic Assamese arising out of large-scale immigration of Bengali Muslims from Bangladesh and consequent fear psychosis of the elite that the political power may slip out from their hands has led to the organization of anti-foreigner movement during the late 1970s and 1980s. The issue of economic underdevelopment of Assam coupled with this identity crisis has led to the formation of ULFA, an ethnic Assamese militant group, which rose to its prominence during the 1990s. The anti-foreigner movement popularly known as Assam movement (1978–85) had not only paralyzed the economy of Assam but also resulted into a huge number of drop outs from schools, colleges, and universities. These youth whose academic carrier was disrupted have enrolled en masse in ULFA to carry forward the perceived cause of social justice. As the Assam movement was principally directed against the immigrant Muslim Bengalis, the Muslim Bengali youth have floated a number of Muslim militant groups like Muslim United Liberation Tigers of Assam (MULTA), Muslim United Liberation Front of Assam (MULFA), Muslim Liberation Army (MLA), Muslim Security Council of Assam (MSCA), Muslim Security Force (MSF), Muslim Tiger Force (MTF), Muslim Volunteer Force (MVF), United Liberation Militia of Assam (ULMA), and United Muslim Liberation Front of Assam (UMLFA) ostensibly to safeguard the interest of the Muslim community in Assam. It is an altogether different issue that the Indian security agencies believe that many of these Islamic militant groups have been floated by ISI of Pakistan as part of its strategy to dismember the NER as a revenge against India's active support in dismembering East Pakistan in 1971.

Be that as it may, as the Assam movement sought to protect the interest of the ethnic Assamese, the single largest ethnic group in Assam, it rang an alarm bell for the other indigenous groups in the state. Immediately after the Assam Accord (1985), the Bodo youth formed BdSF in 1986 which was rechristened as National Democratic Front of Bodoland in 1994 in order to protect the interests of the Bodo community. Taking cue from the trend, Dimasa youth have floated Dimasa National Security Force (DNSF) in 1994 and its offshoot Dima Halim Daogah (DHD) in 1995. Karbi youth organized themselves under the United People's Democratic Solidarity (UPDS) in 1999, ethnic militant group of the Karbis, to safeguard the interest of the Karbi community. The identity dynamics in Assam has also led to the formation of a number of Adhivasi militant groups following the attack on the Santhals by the Bodo militant groups in 1995, and formation of KLO, a militant outfit of the Koch–Rajbongshi community, ostensibly fighting for a separate state combining districts of North Bengal and Lower Assam. All these ethnic militant groups have converted Assam into a killing field where low level of economic development and large-scale unemployment intermingling with the dynamics of social identity driving the youth to join militancy.

The Conflict Trap

India's northeast has long been caught into a conflict trap. The vicious cycle of underdevelopment-livelihood, insecurity-militancy-erosion, destruction, and flight of capital-perpetuation of underdevelopment is in operation in the NER since independence. This vicious cycle gets reinforced through a number of feeder loops specific to a particular society like immigration-identity crisis of the host society-ethnic-militancy-violence- underdevelopment in case of Assam and Tripura, and, nationality aspiration for secession-violence-underdevelopment in case of Nagaland and Manipur.

The state-centric security perception during the early decades of independence did not allow any massive central-sector investment in the region. Like the colonial policy of keeping the Himalayan region as buffer between the British India on the one side and Russia and China on the other, the independent India also appeared to have followed a similar strategy by way of keeping the NER as buffer against China and Pakistan. As per the traditional security approach, the bordering northeastern states were kept inaccessible so that they can act as the natural barriers against any external aggression. In fact, till 1962 Sino-Indian border conflict, development of the NER had become the hostage of traditional approach towards border security. A decade between the Sino-Indian border conflict (1962) and liberation of East Pakistan (1971), intense feeling of territorial insecurity precluded any major investment in the NER as India was not sure whether it could hold the region in case of the simultaneous thrust from China and Pakistan across the Chicken's Neck. By the time Pakistani threat to India's north eastern border melted down following the liberation of East Pakistan and a policy of forward engagement put in place by way of reorganization of the NER in 1972, external security threats were replaced by deteriorating internal security environment with the rebellion of the Nagas, Mizos, and Meiteis getting into momentum. With the proliferation of ethnic militancy in Assam and Tripura during the 1980s, private investment shied away from the region as high risk of the projects has made investment economically non-viable. As most of the states in the NER started developing the syndrome of state fragility since 1980s, most of the state-level public enterprises became dysfunctional. Thus in an era of state-led development during the 1970s and 1980s, the governments in the northeastern states were unable to correct the failure of the market. Since 1990s, as the economic reforms push the states to backstage as the market becomes the driver of growth, the development of the NER has become a problematic as the forces of market could hardly find any links through which they can work. Moreover, there has not been any perceptible change in the business confidence as the risk perceptions still persist at large. Thus the dynamics of external security threats and internal insecurity have caused underdevelopment to perpetuate in the NER since independence.

Economic underdevelopment has eroded the capacity of the northeastern states to provide public goods and welfare services to the people.

Most of the northeastern states have failed to provide quality roads, electricity, transport, health-care services, and education which people value. Faltering by the northeastern states in providing livelihood security by way of job creation for the unemployed youth, and unshackling of other economic opportunities have made the condition of human security vulnerable. The low-growth environment in a multiethnic social setting has widened the horizontal inequality resulting into the proliferation of ethno-national autonomy movements particularly among the ethnic-minority groups. Economic underdevelopment coupled with the psychology of relative deprivation and accentuation of identity crisis, in some cases, has led to the articulation of the demand for secession. As the secessionist movements are viewed to be against the territorial integrity of the Indian state and separatist autonomy movements are viewed to be against the territorial integrity of the subunits, they have been repressed with coercive force resulting into war between the state and the people. Unlike interstate wars, civil wars within the state are long drawn (Collier 2009) and repetitive—the war of the Nagas is going on for more than fifty-five years, rebellion of the Meitei insurgent groups has crossed forty years, the ethnic Assamese militant group (ULFA) is fighting for more than thirty years, and Mizo rebellion took twenty years to settle. All are directed against the state. These wars have attracted tens of thousands of young people most of whom have been the victims of underdevelopment who could otherwise lead a decent life. The long years of violence have not only bled the Indian military machine, but also completely shattered the economy of the NER paving the way for the next generation victims of underdevelopment to join their rank and file. Besides the state versus people war, the conflicting group interests for territorial spaces have led to interethnic violence leading to ethnic cleansing and genocide. The intense feeling of insecurity has led to further proliferation of militant groups as has already been discussed. The multiple layers of conflict have in turn strengthened the forces that help in the perpetuation of underdevelopment.

How to break this conflict trap in the NER? We intend to answer this question in the Chapter 5.

Notes

1. For example, the Naga and Kuki groups collect 'taxes' from all the vehicles plying through both the Imphal–Dimapur–Guwahati and Imphal–Jiribam–

Silchar national highways since 1990. On 6 August 1996, the All Manipur Road Transport Drivers and Motor Workers' Union (AMRTDMWU) and Manipur Truck Owners Welfare Association submitted a memorandum to the union home minister stating that the NSCN (I-M) cadres in the name of Government of Peoples' Republic of Nagaland (GPRN) were collecting 'various taxes' ranging between Rs 1,000 to Rs 10,000 from every vehicles plying along these two highways. In another memorandum on 12 March 1999, the AMRTDMWU sought protection of road transporters and passengers on the highways alleging that the NSCN (I-M) members 'demanding and extorting with receipts in the name of GPRN' from each and every truck as goods tax in the following rates: (*a*) from every gas cylinder truck, Rs 2,000 per trip; (*b*) from every oil tanker, Rs 3,000 per trip; (*c*) all the trucks carrying different goods—trucks carrying iron rods and scrap irons, Rs 3,000 per trip; trucks carrying cement, Rs 1,000 per trip; trucks carrying rice from FCI godown, Rs 500 per trip; trucks carrying essential commodities such as rice, pulses, edible oil, and others, Rs 700 to Rs 800 per trip; trucks carrying sand, Rs 300 per trip. The memorandum also pointed out that the NSCN (I-M) collected road taxes from the vehicles on the basis of Rs 12,000 from every tourist bus, Rs 7,000 from every truck, and Rs 10,000 per annum per agent of gas cylinder (Singh 2011; Tarapot 2005).

2. Singh (2011), Parratt (2005), and Tarapot (2005) have listed a number of cases of shooting by the insurgent groups in Manipur for noncompliance of their dictate for extortion. In 2002, Kanglei Yawol Kanna Lup [KYKL (O)] shot Dr Bedikumar of Regional Institute of Medical Sciences (RIMS) in leg because, it alleged, he had refused to levy its tax of 1.5 per cent on RIMS employees. Again in 2004 the same group shot an officer of the state's horticulture and conservation department in the thigh in pursuance of their demand for no less than Rs 57 lakh from the department. Another incident which shocked everyone was the gunning down of three catholic priests of the Don Bosco Training Centre at Ngariyan hill, about 10km southeast of Imphal on 15 May 15, 2001. The police version was that KYKL (T) was behind the act for not paying the full amount of the huge monetary demand but the outfit denied the charges. Again on 10 November 2005, KYKL exploded a bomb in Imphal city targeting a particular shop for refusing to pay the demand of tax. On 21 October 2005, PREPAK attacked the residence of Arambam Binodini, Joint Director, Department of Tribal Development and Other Backward Classes for failure to meet the deadline for payment of extortion money. On 27 November 2006, the same group locked up main office of Manipur State Agriculture Department at Sanjengthong for refusal to pay money and again on 12 December of the

same year the outfit hurled a bomb at the residence of the Director of Agriculture (Singh 2011). There are many more such incidents. Several senior officials including chief engineer (PWD), S. Binoykumar Singh, chief engineer (PHE), Thingom Ibochouba, Loktak Hydro Electric Project chief engineer, Subhas Chandra Ser, Director (Health services), Surchand Singh, a telecom department engineer, Ambe, Director (tourism), Dasarath Prasad (IAS), executive engineer of Singda Dam project, A.K. Mathur, assistant accounts officer of the project, T.K. Das, a contractor of the project, Phoni Bushan Verma, etc., fell to the bullets of the different underground groups for refusing to concede to their pressures.

3. It is reported that when the stock market in Southeast asia crashed, NSCN (I-M) had lost over Rs 10 crore (Nag 2008).
4. A conservative guesswork suggests that multilayer modes of rent seeking by the militants involves at least 15–20 per cent of the budgetary allocation of the state of Manipur which stands to the tune of Rs 633 crore as per the 2007–8 budgetary expenditure of the state. Thus, at least one-fifth of the budget of the state goes to oil the militancy machine of the state. Assuming half of this amount going for counter-insurgency operations, rent seeking by the state actors and the intermediary agents like the contractors and suppliers, another Rs 317 crore is withdrawn from the productive services. Thus the actual size of the economy gets reduced to one-third due to the combined rent seeking from all quarters (Singh 2011).
5. See 'Nellie Massacre', available at http://en.wikipedia.org/wiki/Nellie_massacre (accessed on 3 July 2011).
6. Ibid.

CHAPTER 5

Breaking the Conflict Trap in India's Northeast

As has already been analysed in the previous chapters, there is no unique causality for the growth of ethnic militancy in the NER. Interlocking of several factors like economic underdevelopment, unemployment, identity crisis, politics of identity, corruption, coercive policy, and above all, state fragility keeps on reinforcing the ethnic conflicts and violence in the NER. As these drivers are embedded in the dynamics of development of the political economy of the societies in northeastern states, coercive approach based on military solution to problems is unlikely to yield the desired result. In fact, security measures need to be backed by the development measures as there is strong interdependence between these two. Policies, schemes, and projects for the fragile areas need to combine the elements of security and development in such a way so that one set of measures can support the other in order to affect a change in the system.

In order to break the conflict trap in the NER, actions may be initiated on the following areas involving multiple agencies acting in different tiers of governance:

1. Promoting economic development
2. Improving the governance
3. Engaging the neighbours
4. Working with the international community

Promoting Economic Development

Vigorous persuasion of economic development is the key for breaking the conflict trap in the NER. Given the peripheral and landlocked position, national framework of development is less likely to be of any benefit for the NER. The first and foremost element for invigorating the process of economic development is to address the predicaments of the region's isolation and landlockedness.

Breaking the Physical Isolation: From Landlocked to Landlinked

Before the partition of the Indian subcontinent in 1947, the NER was linked with the mainland of India through the present-day Bangladesh. The multimodal communication channels between the NER and mainland India used to run through Bangladesh plain. Following the partition, these traditional channels of communication got disrupted making the NER a landlocked territory. In post-partition India, the NER is connected with the mainland through the narrow 'Chicken's Neck'/'Siliguri Corridor' which has widened the road distance between the NER and eastern entry port of India, that is, Kolkata, at least four fold. Although the NER is rich in resources like hydrocarbons, forest, hydroelectricity, and other minerals, high transportation cost did not allow her to grow according to her comparative advantages. The connectivity bottlenecks have made the region perpetually underdeveloped and hence politically volatile. If the development of the NER has to be ensured within the national framework, the only option is to reduce the road distance between the region and mainland India. This calls for the restoration of her traditional routes through Bangladesh. A two-way transit corridor through Bangladesh for the movement of goods and passengers between the NER and mainland India can only address the adverse geographical impact of partition and ensure speedy development of the NER.

Table 5.1 shows the road and railway distance between the important cities of the NES and Kolkata via Chicken's Neck. Table 5.2 shows the same distances via Bangladesh. It may be noted that once transit corridor through Bangladesh is used, the distance between Agartala to Kolkata is reduced by 73 per cent. The people of the state of Tripura will not only

Table 5.1: Distance between Capitals of the Northeastern States and Kolkata via Chicken's Neck

	From	To	Distance and Travel Time			
			Road		*Rail*	
			Distance (in km)	*Travel Time (in hrs)*	*Distance (in km)*	*Travel Time (in hrs)*
1.	Agartala	Kolkata	1,680	170	1,565	120
2.	Silchar	Kolkata	1,407	146	1,368	96
3.	Guwahati	Kolkata	1,081	75	972	48
4.	Shillong	Kolkata	1,181	80	No rail connectivity	
5.	Imphal	Kolkata	1,742	155	No rail connectivity	
6.	Aizwal	Kolkata	1,657	152	No rail connectivity	

Source: Author's calculation based on field survey.

Table 5.2: Distance between Capitals of the Northeastern States and Kolkata via Bangladesh

	From	To	Distance and Travel Time			
			Road		*Rail*	
			Distance (in km)	*Travel Time (in hrs)*	*Distance*	*Travel Time*
1.	Agartala	Kolkata	450	35	No rail connectivity	
2.	Silchar	Kolkata	600	35	Rail connectivity is non-functional	
3.	Guwahati	Kolkata	820	50	No rail connectivity	
4.	Shillong	Kolkata	720	46	No rail connectivity	
5.	Imphal	Kolkata	900	55	No rail connectivity	
6.	Aizwal	Kolkata	800	42	No rail connectivity	

Source: Author's calculation based on field survey.

enjoy lesser transportation cost due to shortening of distance but will also save about 80 per cent travel time (Table 5.3). Like Agartala, whole of the South Assam will also be immensely benefited from the transit facility through Bangladesh in terms of both reduced distance and travel time (Tables 5.3 and 5.4). Similarly both Manipur and Mizoram will

Table 5.3: Travel Time Differential between Capitals of the Northeastern States and Kolkata via Chicken's Neck vis-à-vis Bangladesh (Roadways)

	From	To	Travel Time Road Distance (in hrs)		
			Via Chicken's Neck	Via Bangladesh	Travel Time Differential
1.	Agartala	Kolkata	170	35	135
2.	Silchar	Kolkata	146	35	111
3.	Guwahati	Kolkata	75	50	25
4.	Shillong	Kolkata	80	46	34
5.	Imphal	Kolkata	155	55	100
6.	Aizwal	Kolkata	152	42	110

Source: Author's calculation based on field survey.

Table 5.4: Distance Differential between Capitals of the Northeastern States and Kolkata via Chicken's Neck vis-à-vis Bangladesh

	From	*To*	*Distance* *Road Distance (in km)*		
			Via Chicken's Neck	*Via Bangladesh*	*Distance Differential*
1.	Agartala	Kolkata	1,680	450	1,230
2.	Silchar	Kolkata	1,407	600	807
3.	Guwahati	Kolkata	1,081	820	261
4.	Shillong	Kolkata	1,181	720	461
5.	Imphal	Kolkata	1,742	900	842
6.	Aizwal	Kolkata	1,657	800	857

Source: Author's calculation based on field survey.

also be able to reap a large benefit once the Bangladesh corridor is made operational. For both Manipur and Mizoram, the distance between their respective state capitals to Kolkata will be reduced by about 850 km and travel time will be reduced by about 100 hrs. For Meghalaya, a diversion of traffic from Chicken's Neck route to the Bangladesh (Dawki–Tamabil) route reduces the distance by 461 km and saves travel time by 34 hrs. Although marginal, even it is beneficial for traffic to take route via Bangladesh from Guwahati rather than along the Chicken's Neck as it reduces the distance by 261 km and saves travel time by 25 hrs. Besides these northeastern states, as the traffic from Nagaland and Arunachal Pradesh also moves via Guwahati, they can also avail this marginal benefit if they choose to travel via Bangladesh.

Table 5.5 shows per ton/per km transport cost. It may be noted that the transport cost is a function of distance to be covered. The further the distance, the higher is the transport cost and vice versa. Assuming that transport cost per ton/per km is the same along the Chicken's Neck and route through Bangladesh, a sum of Rs 4,477.20 will be saved if a ton of goods is moved via Bangladesh from Agartala to Kolkata rather than via Chicken's Neck. If 50 per cent of this cost differential is attributed as the transit fee to be accrued to Bangladesh, then business in Agartala will save Rs 2,238.60 for every ton of goods while moved through Bangladesh instead of via Chicken's Neck. This will in turn bring down the cost of living drastically which will promote economic well-being of the people living in the border state of Tripura. The per ton transport cost differentials shown in Table 5.5 reveal that if goods are moved through transit route via Bangladesh immense benefit will also accrue to south Assam region, Manipur, and Mizoram.

As these benefits will also accrue to outbound traffic from the northeastern states to mainland India as well, goods produced within

Table 5.5: Transport Cost Differential between Capitals of the Northeastern States and Kolkata via Chicken's Neck vis-à-vis Bangladesh (Roadways)

	From	*To*	*Road Distance (in Rs)*			
			At per ton/per km	*Via Chicken's Neck per ton*	*Via Bangladesh per ton*	*Transport Cost Differential*
1.	Agartala	Kolkata	3.64	6,115.20	1,638.00	4,477.20
2.	Silchar	Kolkata	3.16	4,446.12	1,896.00	2,550.12
3.	Guwahati	Kolkata	2.06	2,226.86	1,689.20	537.66
4.	Shillong	Kolkata	2.25	2,657.25	1,620.00	1,037.25
5.	Imphal	Kolkata	3.30	5,748.60	2,970.00	2,778.60
6.	Aizwal	Kolkata	3.30	5,468.10	2,640.00	2,828.10

Source: Author's calculation based on field survey.

the region can attain the competitive edge which will then encourage the business to grow according to the comparative advantage of the region.

From the Bangladesh point of view, as the territory of Bangladesh lies between the NER and mainland India, she can make commercial use of her unique location by providing transit services to India. This will be beneficial for Bangladesh at least in two ways. First, in terms of transit fee, which will no doubt be a substantial amount as all the states in the NER heavily depend upon the supply from the mainland. It is approximated (from records available with interstate custom gates) that annually 15 million metric tons of goods move between the NER and mainland India. If this traffic is diverted through Bangladesh as there is strong economic reason to do so, then Bangladesh can earn a hefty amount of transit fee which will be able to substantially neutralize the chronic deficit balance of trade that Bangladesh is experiencing in her merchandize trade with India. Besides this transit fee for interstate movement of goods between the Indian states through Bangladesh, transit fee for international export and import of cargos of the states of the NER would also accrue to Bangladesh once Chittagong port is opened up for them. Moreover improvement in connectivity between the NER and Bangladesh will also boost up the volume of trade between these two regions. Thus, it is a win-win situation for both India and Bangladesh in transforming the NER from landlocked to landlinked. India needs to work out a transit framework that addresses the security interest of Bangladesh as the perceived security threat argument has made political consensus on this issue difficult (Das 2008a). Realising the tremendous liberating implication of this transit corridor for the NER, India can accommodate other economic and military interests of Bangladesh through bilateral framework.

Investing on Connectivity and Infrastructure

The NER is the most poorly connected region in India. Poor connectivity between the region and mainland as well as within the region is the greatest challenge for the promotion of regional development. While the road density for the country stands at 92.72 km/100 sq km (GoI 2010), the same for the region is only 32.13 km/100 sq km (NEC 2006). Within the region, while Tripura has the highest density (65.46 km/100 sq km), the same for Arunachal

Pradesh, Assam, Manipur, Meghalaya, Mizoram, and Nagaland stand at 17.85 km/100 sq km, 44.79 km/100 sq km, 26.33 km/100 sq km, 25.07 km/100 sq km, 22.99 km/100 sq km, and 52.29 km/100 sq km, respectively (NEC 2006). Besides roads, rail connectivity is no better. Except Assam and Tripura, states like Arunachal Pradesh, Manipur, Mizoram, and Nagaland are only symbolically present in the Indian railway map. Meghalaya is yet to find a place in that. While the density of railway route length at the national level stands at 19.21 km/1,000 sq km, the same for Arunachal Pradesh, Assam, Manipur, Meghalya, Mizoram, Nagaland, and Tripura stands at 0.01 km/1,000 sq km, 32.08 km/1,000 sq km, 0.04 km/1,000 sq km, 0.0 km/1,000 sq km, 0.09 km/1,000 sq km, 0.78 km/1,000 sq km, and 4.29 km/1,000 sq km, respectively.[1] Like surface transport, transport network through waterways has also remained underdeveloped.

Although the Brahmaputra and Barak–Surma–Kushiyara–Meghna river systems were extensively used for transport and trade between northeast India and the port of Kolkata during the colonial period, these waterways fell into disuse since the partition of the country. In spite of the fact that the NER has about 1,800 km of river routes that can be used by steamers and large country boats, there exists an Indo-Bangladesh Protocol on Inland Water Transit and Trade signed in 1972, waterways in the NER have remained heavily underutilized. Thus, the development of a multi-modal transportation network across the border, between the region and mainland and within the region, is a sine qua non for ushering in economic development in the NER. In the first case, the process of integration of the economies of northeastern states with the neighbouring South Asian and Southeast Asian economies will be hastened enabling the region to reap the benefits from India's Look East Policy. In the second case, time distance between the region and the mainland India will be reduced breaking the isolation of the region. In the third case, the process of regionalization of the economies of northeastern states will be accelerated leading to the emergence of a division of labour in the sphere of production. The regionalization of market will then strengthen the mutual interdependence of the states and communities facilitating the emergence of a shared multicultural social space which will in turn reduce the intensity of interethnic distrust and hostility.

Next to communication network, the critical input required for the development of an area is the availability of electricity. In spite of being rich in sources of energy, the region is languishing far behind in terms of power generation and consumption. The region is the store house of crude oil (70.46 million tonnes in Assam), natural gas (48,000 million cubic metres in Assam and Tripura), and coal (1,043 mt in Assam, Meghalaya, Arunachal Pradesh, and Nagaland) (Das 2005c). Besides considerable potential for coal-, gas-, and fuel-based energy production, the region is having huge potential for hydropower generation as well. As per the estimate of Central Electricity Authority (CEA), the Brahmaputra basin alone has the potential of 31,857 MW (at 60 per cent load factor) out of the country's total hydropower potential of 84,000 MW (Das 2005a). Very little of this potential has been actualized. As the resource use in the periphery is ordered by the needs of the core, it is only recently with the rise in demand for power in the mainland has led to an impetus for power generation in the NER. Nonetheless, all the northeastern states are power deficit. During 2009–10, the peak deficit in the NER was about 18 per cent (CEA 2010).

For all these years, infrastructure development in the NER was largely determined by the state-centric security perception and defence needs. Security inputs were factored into in making public investment decisions. High-investment projects which cannot be defended from military point of view were either located outside the region or discouraged on security grounds. Road construction activities were guided by strategic requirements. Little efforts were made to reconcile the needs of security to that of development. As a result, markets in the northeastern states remained segregated and potentials remained untapped. It is thus important to realize that neither a security policy undermining the development needs nor a development policy undermining the security needs could possibly succeed in the bordering regions like the NER. A composite policy that views both the requirements as complementary to each other needs to be put in place.

Cross-border Trade and Cooperation as a Strategy of Development of the NER

As the NER shares 98 per cent of her border with the neighbouring countries of Bangladesh, Bhutan, China, and Myanmar, and only about

2 per cent with mainland India, it is only natural that cross-border markets would act for the vent for region's surplus (Das 2000) as the national market centres are far away. This lack of access to market has been one of the main causes for the underutilization of the available resources as well as weak resource industry linkage in the region. The small and segregated internal market of the region has been the major hindrance that makes the better use of her rich natural resources commercially unviable. The resource exploitation here warrants first the scarcity of a particular natural resource product to go up to such a level that can justify the higher price at which it can be supplied in the national market by using the resources from the peripheral states of northeast. As the market signals emanating from the operation of the national economy are not strong enough to bring all the resources of the region, except critical ones, into immediate use, the role of the markets across the border comes in handy. Here lies the rationale to look beyond the framework of the national economy and the state-centric mindset while formulating the development strategy for the border areas like the NER (Das 2005c).

The model of market-led growth initiated through economic reforms is generating growth only in those areas having comparative advantages in terms of transport cost, transaction cost, and labour cost. Firms tend to locate their operations in those areas which help them to remain competitive in the market. As the peripheral areas are located far away from the main centres of national markets and international connectivity, suffer from high transportation costs and transaction costs, and lack skilled labour, market forces are unlikely to boost growth in them (Das and Singh 2010).

In order to counter the imperfections of the market forces, nation states are trying to develop these areas through higher resource allocation in terms of plan allocation and centrally sponsored schemes. In India, since 1996, the central government has focused on New Initiative for North East. Under this initiative, 10 per cent of annual budgetary provisions of all central ministries/departments are earmarked for the development of the NER. A 'non-lapsable pool of fund' has also been created to ensure transfer of fund from the centre to the NER, which amounts to Rs 1,500 crore annually. In order to oversee the development activities in the NER, a separate department called Department of Development of North Eastern Region has also been created at the centre (Das 2005b). The GoI had also framed a separate industrial policy for the NER in 1997, which aims at providing infrastructural facilities, creating growth centres and free tax zones as well as supplying various incentives in order to promote industrial development in the region. Besides these economic measures, political measures were also taken up to engage various militant secessionist groups in peace talks in order to restore business confidence in the region. Efforts are also being made to improve the quality of governance by coupling accountability to resource transfer (Das 2005b).

As far as the Indian experience with state-sponsored peripheral growth efforts are concerned, it has been observed that this has led to some sort of dependency syndrome. States in India's northeast hardly take initiatives to utilize and expand their resource bases for sustainable growth. The political economy in these states revolves around as to how to receive additional central grants instead of generating additional wealth through enhancing their resource-use efficiency. Moreover, clientalization of real politic in these states has led to the use of central grants as state privileges by the politicians in order to solidify their support bases. This has encouraged cronyism and rent seeking to seep into the state structure leading to frustrating growth experiences in the peripheries. All these add to transaction costs of doing business in the peripheral regions (Das and Singh 2010).

Besides higher transaction costs, even if state-sponsored peripheral growth efforts succeed to create better infrastructure through public investments, they cannot reduce the geographical distance of the peripheries from the main centres of trade and commerce of a nation. The effect of creation of infrastructure on the reduction of transport costs will only be minimal. As a result, the strategy of growth through industrialization will have limited impact in boosting the economies of the peripheral regions. Thus, nation states have limited options to infuse growth in the peripheral regions as the market-led growth models within the framework of nation state can hardly be of any use in this regards (Das and Singh 2010).

As has already been discussed, neither the market-led national growth model nor the state-sponsored peripheral growth model is effective for the landlocked frontier regions which lie far away from the national heartland. Both national and international private investments shy away of these regions due to high transportation costs, transaction costs, and production costs. Moreover, as the large investment decisions are often informed of security considerations, state-centric security perceptions of the nation states which often perceive these frontier regions as vulnerable also stands on the way of installation of large projects in these regions.

As a result, 'border trade' may be viewed as a strategic tool for the long-term development of the frontier areas. As has already been discussed elsewhere (Das 2005c, 2006b), the task of developing these areas is easier through cross-border cooperation than through national efforts alone. A three-step development strategy may be chalked out in order to forge triadic linkages among resource base, production structure, and trade in the frontier regions.

As the first step, these areas may be opened up for 'border area trade' which will enable people across the border to exchange locally produced goods within a specified radius. This will ease out the life of the border population. This intrinsic value of border trade over time will lead to the emergence of instrumental value (Das 2002c). Once the 'border area trade' takes root, people-to-people contact, flow of information as well as development of road connectivity across the border will enable both the regional governments to open up transit trade as the second step.

Transit trade will call for putting up the required infrastructural facilities and regulatory framework on both sides of the border. The border trading points will be focused on both regional and national businesses. Depending upon the complementarity or competitive resource structure, the transit trade will first establish dyadic linkages between trade and local resource mobilization across the border. This will, in turn, lead to the establishment of road connectivity between the border points and regional/national business centres.

As production at far-away places and the transportation of the goods to far-away markets will be less cost effective, some firms will be trying to locate small plants within the border province. This may take the form of branching out or collaborative ventures with the local or regional businesses. The national governments may establish free-trade zones along borders and encourage the provincial governments to establish export processing zones in the border towns/provincial business centres.

The government/business interest may encourage joint ventures to take root in these border towns particularly in areas of common interest. As the natural resource base, river routes, vegetation, etc., cut across the political boundaries, there exists a common ground for cooperation, which will enable the people of both sides to reap the benefits through joint efforts. Once this cross-border development cooperation takes shape, the triadic linkages among resource base, production structure, and trade will be established and the development process will acquire momentum in the border province (Das and Singh 2010). State-sponsored peripheral growth efforts will be able to use the institution of market in a better way if the cross-border markets are integrated and cross-border synergies are harnessed for mutual benefits.

Border trade is a multidimensional policy instrument having a number of implications for the welfare of the people living across the border as well as deeper and wider political implications for bilateral relations between nations sharing the border. First and foremost is the intrinsic value of border trade as it eases lives of people living in the bordering regions. Border-area trade not only enables people across the border to exchange necessities in terms of goods and services, but also allows knowledge, information, and ideas to flow across the communities, enhances security as people get to know each other better, learn to live together, and share each other's life experiences. Second, as the national growth models are hardly effective in far-flung border regions, border trade may be used as a strategy for frontier development through mobilizing the cross-border synergies. Third, nations can better address the grievances of the border population arising out of sluggish growth and the problems of regional income disparities that often lead to the growth of secessionist tendencies among the border communities. Fourth, vibrant border trade leads to better border management as the borders remain regularly in focus. Fifth, in case of disputed border, the instrument of border trade may be used as a CBM between the nations as has been argued by Singh (2010). Sixth, as far as India–China border is concerned, instrument of border trade might be used in order to facilitate the transition of

LAC into official international border in case both the nations agree to arrive at such negotiation in future.

Already a symbiotic growth model is in the making between the NER and Bangladesh due to complementarity between the resource structure of the NER and demand structure of Bangladesh. In fact, most of the cement industries in Bangladesh draw limestone from the hills of Meghalaya. Similarly, a significant part of the coal extracted in the mines in Meghalaya finds its market in Bangladesh. Besides, minerals, the NER also exports agro-horticultural products, and forest-based products to Bangladesh. In turn, a substantial part of the imports of manufacturing goods of Tripura comes from Bangladesh. The bricks, cement, stone chips which are imported by Tripura are produced in Bangladesh using coal, limestone, and boulders of Meghalaya. Similarly, synthetic drinks, spice powder, wooden furniture, cellular rubber, and a number of processed food items that the NER imports from Bangladesh are produced by the latter using the agro-horticultural inputs originated in the former (Barbhuiya 2011). Thus, the resources of the NER combined with the markets in Bangladesh have created a growth dynamic which has generated income, employment, and investment opportunities across the border. In contrast, the trade that flows across the NER–Myanmar border has failed to forge any organic link with the local economies perhaps due to their similar resource base. However, the transit trade has also created income and employment opportunities albeit at a limited scale. Thus, public policies need to be designed to promote the cross-border trade and cooperation to turn the geopolitical disadvantages of the bordering regions into geo-economic advantages. This calls for opening up of as many borderland ports as possible along the international borders with Bangladesh, Bhutan, China, and Myanmar and India's engagement with the neighbours for mobilizing the synergies across the border for development of the border areas. As the state-centric security perspective and development programmes do not meet at the borders, their non-complementarity results into social unrest among the people living therein in many of the nation states making the border perpetually security sensitive. It is thus important for the nation states to transcend the state-centric approach and adopt a regional framework of cooperation that combines both security and development interests for mutual benefit.

Securitization of Development through Involving Community-based Organizations

While the integration of the economies of the NER with the markets across the border will ease out the problems of market access, transit corridor through and access to sea ports of Bangladesh will address the problems of landlockedness, these external opportunities will be of little use in infusing the growth momentum in the local economies unless there is a change in the agency of development. As the state as an agency has failed, involvement of Community-based Organizations (CBOs) in carrying out the development agenda at the grass roots might be seen as the best fit, politically viable alternative model which would be effective in conflict-ridden NER. The traditional social institutions which play an important role in maintaining semblance of peace and tranquillity within the community might be incorporated in the chain of delivery system of public goods and agency of public works along with NGOs and local self governments. As the development projects are the prime source of extortion, their decentralization will certainly reduce the chance of siphoning the fund for militancy. At the grassroots, CBOs will decide the resource allocation and oversee the implementation of the projects. Executing agencies should be made accountable to these CBOs. This will put the responsibilities for the success of the development schemes and projects directly on the people concerned who will be the beneficiaries of these development activities. This will shift the war from state-versus-militant groups to state versus people. The target of the militants' gun would get multiplied and in the process would miss the object-giving development a chance to survive (Singh 2011). Public utilities may be created by the state and handover their management to the CBOs. Public services like education and healthcare, if provided through the CBOs, would be more accessible to people particularly in remote and rural areas. The CBOs might also be entrusted the responsibilities of community policing, which in turn can play an important role in conflict prevention leading to strengthening the state–society relationship (World Bank 2011).

Creation of Jobs

Job creation should be the cardinal principle of public investment in conflict-ridden societies in the NER. The sectors having higher employment elasticity should get the larger share of resources. Investment and entrepreneurial initiatives need to be promoted through the institutions of cooperatives. As the private entrepreneurial initiatives are more vulnerable in a conflict zone like the NER, collectivized initiatives are likely to succeed. Institutional credit and government support need to be integrated with the cooperative initiatives. These cooperative organizations would act as an agency of transformation of the economy of the NER from tradition to modernity (Singh 2011). The CBOs and the various occupational cooperatives might be encouraged to promote labour intensive productions having links with regional and national value chain. National and international private-sector investments might be provided with guarantee by both the state and CBOs so that they can operate in an environment free from risks of violence and intimidation. Once employment opportunities open up, this will dry up the pipeline of recruitment of youth and help in the reduction of cycles of violence in subsequent period.

Improving the Governance

Besides breaking the cycle of underdevelopment and militancy through invigorating economic development of the NER, simultaneous efforts are also called for the improvement in governance.

Federal Solution and Politics of Accommodation

One of the tasks of good governance is to manage, mediate, and resolve social conflict. Basic source of conflict in multiethnic NER is embedded in interethnic relationship and relative position of an ethno-social group in the identity matrix within the political boundary of a particular subunit. As the relative strength of a community to influence the decision-making process in an electoral democracy depends on its relative electoral strength, the ethnic majority enjoys a kind of political hegemony over the ethnic minorities. Unequal access to power results into horizontal inequality among the different ethno-social groups. The laggard minority communities then articulate their grievances and demand for political autonomy and/or measures for positive discrimination in order to protect their respective community interests. The separatist demand for statehood (subunit status) within the Indian Union by the Bodos, Karbis, and Dimasas in Assam fall in this category. These are identity-based autonomy movements. In fact, in a larger context, both the secessionist Naga and Meitei movement in Nagaland and Manipur, respectfully, also fall under the same category. However, the movement by the tribals in Tripura against the immigrant Hindu Bengalis and ethnic Assamese in Assam against the immigrant Muslim Bengalis are basically movements for the protection and preservation of identities. In case of Tripura, the tribals have already become the minority and lost the political power to the immigrant Hindu Bengalis and in case of Assam's Muslim Bengalis have evolved as a formidable force in the political power matrix as they constitute about 30 per cent of the population. The fear of being swept over by the non-tribal, á la Tripura, has led the tribal groups in Meghalaya, Nagaland, Mizoram, and Arunachal Pradesh to pose a violent anti-nontribal position which keeps interethnic schism to dominate the social space.

In a multiethnic social environment, it is important for the state to promote the politics of accommodation rather than politics of exclusion. Federal solution to ethnic aspiration for autonomy has already proved to be an effective option. Formation of Autonomous Council under the Sixth Schedule of the Indian constitution has successfully restored peace in Tripura and prevented escalation of violence in Assam and Meghalaya. Use of this tool in Manipur may provide a clue to the resolution of Meitei–Naga conflict in Manipur where Nagas residing in the hills aspire to merge with their brethren in Nagaland and Meiteis aspire to protect the historically evolved territorial boundary of the state (see Das 2006a for a detailed discussion on Meitei–Naga conflicting interest). Devolution and decentralization of state power is a better option than suppressing the autonomy aspiration of the minorities that may result into long-drawn bloody civil war for secession or separation (World Bank 2011). In fact, it is either by secession or separation that a minority assumes the status of majority in the newly carved out territory (Raju 1996). However, as the NER is the home of innumerable ethnic categories, Sixth Schedule type federal solution also bears the probable danger of social disintegration.

Much of the demand for political autonomy by the minority ethnic groups would have withered away had democracy worked at the grassroots level. Thus, it is a far better option to make democracy work at the grassroots level so that grievances of the minorities could be attended through the functioning of the local self governments. As the demand for political autonomy by the ethnic minorities often results from non-mitigation of a set of grievances, for example, reservation of jobs, recognition of a dialect/language, political representation, and so on, the state can resolve the autonomy issue by negotiating and accommodating the specific demands of the minorities within the existing framework. Moreover, creation of an upper chamber of the state legislature and accommodation of the representatives of the ethnic minorities in it might be another option for the multiethnic states in the NER to promote the politics of inclusion.

Action on Corruption

Corruption erodes the legitimacy of a regime. Besides its growth decelerating effects (Akcay 2006), corruption in public offices gives birth to grievances particularly among the victims who in turn may resort to violent means seeking social justice. In extreme cases, corruption may render a country ungovernable and lead to political instability and conflict (Bottelier 1998). The credibility of the power elite in northeastern states like Assam, Manipur, and Nagaland is at stake due to high incidence of corruption in public offices. The governments of northeastern states may institute Public Expenditure Tracking Survey in order to ensure that the allocated fund reaches to the target groups (World Bank 2011). Traditional social institutions and CBOs might be involved in executing public works and empowered to monitor the public-welfare expenditure. Public decision-making and public-expenditure information might be made transparent at the local level. Use of information technology in public services can also rein in rent seeking activities to a large extent. The best example as to what the use of information technology can do to weed out rent seeking is Indian Railways. Before the launch of online booking and reservation services, various forms of bribe rackets used to operate in the system and people had to pay additional illegal charges for getting railway reservations. Once the system became online, transparency has helped in the elimination of bribery for this service. Like the Indian Railways, the northeastern states may use the information technology to clean up the public offices that will lead to the restoration of people's confidence on the regime.

Replacing Coercive Approach by Security-enhancing Approach

States or sovereign powers across nations have a tendency to treat 'militant political movements' or 'insurgency' of all sheds as a single category. Needless to say, this perception is state-centric in nature. It essentially stems from the idea of indivisibility of the sovereignty of the state. As these movements pose a challenge to the authority and legitimacy of the existing socio-political and economic order having approval of the state, challenging the same amounts to challenging the sovereign power of the state. This state-centric threat perception leads to the formulation of uniform response primarily in terms of coercive measures—formulation of coercive laws—deployment of security forces—in order to combat the militant movements. Military solution precedes political dialogue. While force fails to yield results, other options are considered.

Let us first recognize that all social movements are the responses of collectivities—ethnic group, tribe, nationality, class, or religious group—seeking redress of certain issues that they feel will enhance the welfare of the members of the collectivity, either by protecting them from negative consequences of the issues or by positive gains that will accrue out of their resolution. The similarity of social predicaments that the individuals face acts as motivating force for them. They unite and form collective platform as the individuals realize that it is not possible to get rid of the predicaments through lone efforts. The very nature of the relationship between individual and the collectivity to which he belongs to motivates him to respond to the cause of the group unless his level of consciousness transcends the cultural boundary of the collectivity.

As individuals are born and brought up within a cultural environment created by the collectivity, the expansion of collective space enlarges the space for an individual to grow and achieve the goals. Similarly, the individual perceives threat when the space for collectivity is curtailed. This organic relationship between an individual and collectivity leads to personalization of collective interests and motivates and draws the individual into social movement.

In fact, the social movement is the symbol of a vibrant society. A society facing multidimensional challenges is prone to multi-directional social movements. As long as the movements follow the rules of the game set by the ongoing socio-political order, resolution of conflicts, and realization of goals are sought through and within the given socio-political order. In fact, accommodation of people's interests through modification and upgradation of the ongoing socio-political framework is a continuous process. Everywhere the art of polity management faces the challenges of adapting change for status quo. Bureaucratic organization like the state is rule governed. Rules routinize the functioning of state apparatus. Changes need to be internalized and routinized. Hence, bureaucratic-polity management encourages status quo and resists change. Thus, a contradiction arises: while a social movement seeks change, the state seeks to continue with the status quo.

Every social movement has a history. Discontent against a particular order gathers momentum with the passage of time. A movement initially seeks to redress the grievances through peaceful means. It mobilizes the members by sensitizing them about the consequences of the issues and the benefits of the goals set by it. Even the revolutionary movements begin to mobilize the masses based on achievable goals within the given order. They launch a series of democratic movements in order to rally the masses under their banner. They conduct democratic movements as rehearsals wherein volunteers are trained, educated, tested, and prepared for final showdown. Thus, for revolutionary movements, even though the ultimate goal is extra-constitutional, they go by steps identifying the issues that can be redressed through constitutional means. Small victories strengthen their hands and enable them to mobilize masses to achieve larger goals.

No movement adopts violent course of action since inception. In most cases, the strategy of violence is adopted as the last resort. Militant organizations are the extreme manifestations, which are often formed by the splinter groups of movements. Very often, the failure of democratic conflict resolution mechanism encourages the formation of such groups. At times, lengthy and frustrating conflict gives birth to splinter groups that take recourse in militancy (Das 2006a).

These social dynamics of the emergence of militancy are often overlooked while coercive approach is adopted in dealing with them.

The Naga movement slipped into underground in the face of state coercion during the mid-1950s. The Meitei militancy was the result of a long neglect towards the democratic movement in support of their legitimate demand for statehood of Manipur that lasted for twenty two years (1950–72) (Das and Singh 2009). The Mizo Rebellion (1966–86) was the reaction against the failure of the state to protect the interest of the Mizos during the famine in 1959. The secessionist movement of ULFA took root in Assam as the democratic movements for development held during 1950s and 1960s were not attended. The TNV revolted during the 1980s as the democratic persuasion by the tribals of Tripura to protect their identity and interest on the face of large-scale immigration of Hindu Bengalis from erstwhile East Pakistan met with failure. Had these movements been consulted and the insecurities faced by the people were addressed, the NER would not have become the second soft underbelly of the Indian state today.

The fact that coercive measures become counterproductive in violence prevention is evident from the people's reaction against the imposition and continuation of the Armed Forces Special Power Act (AFSPA) 1958 in Manipur in 1980. Armed with this Act, the security forces in Manipur had unleashed a reign of terror by way of arresting, killing, and raping the women in the name of counter-insurgency operation. Following the incident of alleged rape and killing of a young woman, Monorama Devi, by the Assam Rifles personnel in July 2004, a strong people's movement was organized under the leadership of Apunba Lup, which united thirty-two women, students, and civic organizations. Perhaps the first time in the history, a group of women protested naked in front of the headquarters of the Assam Rifles holding up a banner displaying 'Indian Army, Rape Us.' This shows the intensity of public anger against the coercive measures of the security forces. In fact India's security interest in northeastern border stands at odd to the interest of the Meitei nationalism in Manipur.

The Act, however, instead of curbing insurgency has rather put more oil in the fire. The army's uncontrolled actions often leading to human rights violation had created a fear psychosis among the people in general and youth in particular. This has further escalated the feeling of hatred against the Indian state (represented by the Indian army and other security forces) (Singh 2011), which, in turn, as confessed by one of the top militant leader, has motivated the youth to join the rank and file of militancy in Manipur (Bisheswar 1986: 48–9). Thus, conflict-prevention policies should not be based only on coercive approach without factoring into the social dynamics behind the emergence of such conflicts in the first place. A security enhancing policy might work better for prevention of violence. As human rights are essential element of human security, protecting these rights rather than trampling them would make anti-militancy measures politically acceptable.

Building Inclusive-enough Coalition

Conflict resolution in a multiethnic social environment requires building of inclusive-enough coalition. As the interethnic interests are often conflicting, peacemaking with one group may create hostility with the others and in the process may ultimately derail the whole peace initiative. The Shillong Accord signed in 1975 between the GoI and NNC failed to resolve the Naga movement as a number of key players among the Nagas were left outside. The Assam Accord signed in 1985 between the GoI and AASSU has triggered the Bodo movement as the interest of the Bodos was not addressed. Similarly the Bodo Accord signed in 1993 triggered Adhivasi militancy as the interest of the Santhals living in Bodoland Territorial Council (BTC) area was not addressed.

It is, thus, important to evolve a consensus among different stakeholders associated with a conflict in order to gain legitimacy of a particular solution. Apart from the forces that spearhead the agitation for the resolution of a particular problem, the charter of proposed agreement might be shared with the different civil society organizations, political parties, private business, and groups and agencies which might be negatively affected. A broad-based consultation would not only provide a sense of sharing but also improve the quality of decision-making. Taking the stakeholders at different levels into confidence would provide the necessary resilience to the solution.

Avoiding Peace Traps

The pace of the peace-building process has immense bearing on the prevention of conflict and violence. A number of ethnic militant groups in the northeastern states have signed ceasefire agreement with the central and/or state governments with a hope for the resolution of their core demands. But the snail's pace of the progress of negotiations and poor scope for rehabilitation have already generated a deep frustration among the surrendered militants. The NSCN (I-M) signed the ceasefire agreement with the central government on 1 August 1997. Since then it is being renewed periodically. The peace process that has been going on for more than thirteen years is yet to fathom out a common framework for resolution even after sixty rounds of talk between the NSCN (I-M) leadership and GoI. The UPDS signed a similar ceasefire agreement with the central government on 23 May 2002. After six rounds of talk with the Government of Assam and GoI representatives, the militant group pulled out of the talk as they realized that the government representatives are not willing to address the core issue, that is, upgrading the autonomous district of Karbi Anglong into a full-fledged state under India Union. The DHD has also signed a ceasefire agreement with the central government on 1 January 2003. In spite of repeated appeal from the leadership of the group, even after eight years, the peace talk has not yet been started. The NDFB signed a similar ceasefire agreement with both the Government of Assam and GoI on 25 May 2005, but the formal peace talk is yet to begin.

As per the ceasefire agreement, the members of the militant group entering into the agreement have to stay in designated camps set up by the state governments under the supervision of the security agencies till the completion of the talk. There are a number of such designated camps in Assam, Nagaland, and Manipur. One can only imagine as to how hundreds of youth who used to challenge the might of the Indian Army are languishing in them year after year. A majority of them are suffering from deep frustration due to the tardy progress of the peace talk. In some cases, many of them chose to go back to underground in order to renew their crusade against the state. In Meghalaya, a group of ALMA cadres who surrendered in 1994 slipped to underground again on being frustrated with their rehabilitation and formed People's Liberation Front of Meghalaya (PLF–M), a new militant group, to fight for a separate state for the Garos. In Mizoram, a group of HPC, who surrendered following the signing of Memorandum of Settlement (MoS) with the Government of Mizoram in 1994, chose to take up the gun again due to the tardy progress of the implementation of the agreement and formed Hmar People's Convention (Democratic) (HPC–D) to fight for a homeland of the Hmars.

Although the scale and intensity of violence in the NER in general and Assam in particular has come down substantially in recent years due to engagement of the dreaded militant groups in the peace building, inadequate rehabilitation of the surrendered militants, and poor pace of progress of the peace talks may aggravate the situation in future. It is thus important for the governments in the NER as well as central government to devise effective confidence-building measures in order to prevent the recurrence of violence. Effective rehabilitation packages may be worked out with the help of NGOs and private business. Besides arranging training for the surrendered militants according to their ability and interest, the thriving private-security service providers may be encouraged to employ them as they are already trained in dealing with arms and ammunition. They may be trained in security service providing business modules and employed in guarding government establishments and other public-sector installations.

Besides effective rehabilitation, governments should establish their sincerity in addressing the core issues raised by the different militant groups. Of course, it is not easy to find solution particularly when conflicting interethnic interests are involved. Moreover, when conceding to the demands of one group is likely to open the Pandora's Box while others join the chorus. What is important is to carry the talk forward and expose the negotiating group to the complex consequences that might arise. Building inclusive-enough coalition by way of incorporating the other stakeholders step by step into the peace dialogue and making the negotiation transparent so that civil society at large can also enrich the peace building process in terms of suggesting probable alternatives can go a long way in evolving a compromise solution. This consensus-oriented approach, albeit lengthy, would make all the stakeholders a party to the decision who will not have any moral locus standi to oppose the same. The hardliners, if any, can be easily isolated and bracketed. Instead of building inclusive-enough coalition, if peace negotiation is restricted between the rebel group and the government, the delay, which is only natural as no government wants to risk its electoral fortune, on the part of the government, will be interpreted as intentional and against the interest of the rebel movement. In that case, militants might perceive their position as transformation from a situation of conflict trap to a situation of peace trap. This growing perception among the surrendered militants staying in different designated camps in the northeastern states needs to be addressed by state activism otherwise return of peace might remain only illusory.

Engaging the Neighbours: Reducing the External Stresses

The resolution of violence in many countries is beyond the capacity of the nation state. Nation state alone cannot address the problem as the sphere of operation of the militants transcends the territorial boundary of the nation. Militant groups, while aided and supported by the countries across the border, can wage a long war against their government. In such a situation, a regional cooperation and common initiative can only promote peace. The World Bank (2011) has underlined the importance of regional cooperation in mitigation of conflict and violence in Africa.

Internal insecurity arising out of the operation of ethnic militant groups in the NER is, to a large extent, linked with the political dynamics in South Asia. Both the fronts—Jammu and Kashmir and the NER—where militancy is active for long, share international land border with the neighbouring countries. While Jammu and Kashmir shares her border with Pakistan and China, the NER shares it with Bangladesh, Bhutan, China, and Myanmar. As much of the borders are porous, militant groups operate across the international boundaries. They establish camps across the border, train their cadres, and send bands to sneak in for operation and then sneak out. In fact, borders provide them the necessary shield against the Indian security forces. As a result, without regional cooperation, it is not possible for the Indian state to stop the subversive activities of the militant groups.

The fact that regional cooperation can play a decisive role in violence prevention is evident from India–Bhutan cooperation on security in 2003. While India addressed the security concern of Bhutan arising out of anti-monarchy movement by the Lhotsampas (Nepali-speaking people settled in Bhutan) during the 1990s, Bhutan reciprocated in return addressing Indian security concern arising out operation of the NER rebel groups from her soil by way of launching Operation All Clear, a joint operation of the Indian and Bhutanese Army, in 2003.

This operation had cleared thirteen camps of ULFA, twelve camps of NDFB, and five camps of KLO inside Bhutan where about 3,000 militants have taken shelter since early 1990s.

A similar regional cooperation between India and Bangladesh has resulted into a huge peace dividend for the NER while Bangladesh helped India in arresting the top leaders of ULFA, NDFB, and UNLF during 2009–10. These arrests have significantly strengthened the peace-building process in the region. It may not be out of place to mention that India also helped Bangladesh by way of facilitating the surrender of the Shanti Bahini, a Chakma militant group, in 1997. These bilateral cooperation exhibit that addressing each other's security concerns is mutually beneficial for both the regional partners.

Similar ground for regional cooperation between India and Myanmar will be of immense mutual benefit. As both sides of Indo-Myanmar border are infested with ethnic militancy, drug trade, arms smuggling, addressing each other's security concerns, and cooperation for development through mobilizing cross-border synergies will be of mutual interest for both India and Myanmar. In the same vein, both China and India can better address the issues of underdevelopment and ethnic militancy in the former's southwest region and latter's northeast region if a policy of cross-border cooperation is adopted. Indeed, the task of development of these areas is easier through cross-border cooperation than through national efforts alone (Das 2005b).

Thus, regional cooperation for cross-border development can only integrate the interest of both the partners. This can be done by way of promoting cross-border trade, sharing resources, promoting people to people contact, promoting cross-border interaction of business, profession, and administration. The process will not only be liberating for the landlocked bordering people but also be helpful towards the development of structural interdependence between the areas across the border. Initiation of interstate development projects in bordering areas will make the neighbouring countries a partner of development and create leverage for containing cross-border militancy (Das 2011).

Working with the International Community: Defining the Right to Self-determination

There is a built-in incentive in the international legal principles for the minorities in a country to demand secession from the central government. Basic *et al.* (2003) examine the limitations of international legal principles of self-determination and territorial integrity of the state and analyse as to how the different interpretations of these concepts can induce the actors in secession crises to engage in violent conflicts to further their goals rather than to seek peaceful resolution of their differences.

Article (1) of both the International Covenant on Economic, Social and Cultural Rights and the International Covenant on Civil and Political Rights states: 'All people have the right to self-determination. By virtue of the right they freely determine their political status and freely pursue their economic, social, and cultural development.' In the context of decolonization, the General Assembly subsequently expanded the meaning of self-determination that implies a right to political independence (Basic *et al.* 2003). The militant groups in the NER like NSCN (I-M), ULFA, and UNLF interpret this right to self-determination as right to political independence through secession without any reference as to whether this right is equally applicable for the postcolonial as well as non-colonial pre-existing states or not.

Article 2(4) of the United Nations Charter protects the territorial integrity of any state against any threat or use of force as principle of international law. All states are viewed as sovereign equals and their territorial basis of sovereignty is guaranteed. All sorts of interference in the territorial jurisdiction of a sovereign state are prohibited as per the principles of international law. As a result, the secessionist claims that involve political independence violate the principle of territorial integrity of a state as enshrined in the principle of international law.

Thus, while the interpretation of right to self-determination as a right to political independence encourages the ethnic minorities to wage war against the central government, the principle of territorial integrity of state justifies the acts of suppression of the secessionist movements by the government. Thus the interplay of these two principles of international law has been a major source of violence across the globe including India's NER.

These two apparently contradictory principles of international law can be reconciled if the political meaning of right to self-determinism stands for right to self-governance. Ethnic or religious minorities can enjoy the right to self-governance without seceding from the existing state. The interpretation of right to self-determination in terms of broad and comprehensive senses including autonomy, devolution, power sharing, and federalism in all its forms instead of narrow focus on political independence will certainly discourage the ideology of secessionism. The central government of India through its representatives at the United Nations needs to sensitize the international community the importance of removing the ambiguities in the meaning of the concept of self-determination.

Note

1. See 'Railway Infrastructure in North East'. Available at http://db.nedfi.com/content/railways-0 (accessed on 16 December 2011).

Bibliography

Akiner, Shirin. 2010. 'Conflict and Postconflict in Tajikstan', in Necla Tschirgi, Michael S. Lund, and Francesco Mancini (eds), *Security and Development: Searching for Critical Connections*. Boulder, CO: Lynne Rienner, pp. 339–86.

Aidt, Toke S. 2009. 'Corruption, Institutions, and Economic Development', *Oxford Review of Economic Policy*, 25(2): 271–91.

Akcay, Selcuk. 2006. 'Corruption and Human Development', *Cato Journal*, 26(1): 29–48.

Bandopadhyaya, Jayantanuja. 1991. *The Making of India's Foreign Policy*, reprint. New Delhi: Allied Publishers.

Banerjee, Nirmalya. 2005. 'Army Keeping Vigil on Nepal Maoist-KLO-Ulfa Nexus', *The Times of India*, Guwahati, 3 January. Available at http://timesofindia.indiatimes.com/articleshow/msid-979153,flstry-1.cms (accessed on 16 November 2011).

Barbhuiya, Shelly. 2011. 'Indo-Bangladesh Bilateral Trade Relations: With Special Reference to Border Trade of North-East India', PhD dissertation, mimeo, NIT, Silchar.

Bardhan, Pranab. 1997. 'Corruption and Development: A Review of Issues', *Journal of Economic Literature*, XXXV(September): 1320–46.

Barooah, Nirode K. 1990. *Gopinath Bardoloi, Indian Constitution and Centre State Relations, 1940–1950*. Guwahati, Assam: Publication Board.

Barua, Sanchet. 2008. 'Politician-Separatists Nexus: A Dangerous Cocktail', Navhind Times.com. Available at http://www.navhindtimes.com/story.php?story=2008102823 (accessed on 11 August 2000).

Baruah, Amit. 2001. 'Vietnam for Dynamic ASEAN-Indian Ties', *The Hindu*, 10 January. Available online at http://hindu.com/thehindu/2001/01/10/stories/05101348.htm (accessed on 16 November 2011).

Baruah, Sanjib. 1999. *India against Itself*. New Delhi: Oxford University Press.

Basic, Nedzad, David Goetze, and Charles Anthony Smith. 2003. 'Secession Crises, Human Welfare and Conflict Resolution', *Conflict, Security & Development*, 3(2): 185–209.

Bhaumik, Subir. 1996. *Insurgent Crossfire*. New Delhi: Lancer.

———. 1997. 'The External Linkages in Insurgency in India's Northeast', in B. Pakem (ed.), *Insurgency in North East India*, New Delhi: Omsons Publications, pp. 89–100.

Bhuyan, Arun Chandra and Sibopada De (eds). 1999. *Political History of Assam, vol. II, 1920–1939*, 2nd edition. Guwahati, Assam: Publication Board.

Bisheswar, Nameirakpam. 1986. *The Last Expression on My Death Bed*. Imphal: Pax Publication.

Borner, Silvio, Frank Bodmer, and Markus Kobler. 2003. *Institutional Efficiency and Its Determinants: The Role of Political Factors in Economic Growth*. Paris: Organisation for Economic Co-operation and Development (OECD).

Bottelier, Pieter. 1998. 'The Social and Economic Costs of Corruption'. Available at www.icclr.law.ubc.ca/Publications/Reports/bott_pap.pdf (accessed on 5 July 2011).

Brecher, M. and J. Wilkenfeld. 1990. *Crisis, Conflict and Instability*. Oxford: Pergamon Press.

Brinkerhoff, Jennifer M. 2011. 'Diasporas and Conflict Societies: Conflict Entrepreneurs, Competing Interests or Contributors to Stability and Development?' *Conflict, Security and Development*, 11(2): 115–43.

Business Standard. 1 October 1997. 'Assam Tea Industry in a Tizzy over Brewing Storm'. Available at http://www.business-standard.com/india/news/assam-tea-industry-intizzy-over-brewing-storm/59912/ (accessed on 16 November 2011).

Carment, David, Stewart Prest, and Yiagadeesen Samy. 2010. *Security, Development, and the Fragile State: Bridging the Gap between Theory and Policy*. London: Routledge.

Comptroller and Auditor General (CAG). 2007. 'Audit Report (Revenue), Assam, for the Year 2006–2007'. Available at http://www.cag.gov.in/html/cag_reports/assam/rep_2007/rev_cont.htm (accessed on 26 June 2011).

———. 2009. 'Audit Report (Revenue), Manipur, for the Year 2008–2009'. Available at www.cag.gov.in/html/cag_reports/manipur/rep_2009/civil_chap4.pdf (accessed on 26 June 2011).

Census of India. 2001. 'Primary Census Abstract', Nedfi databank. Available at http://db.nedfi.com/ (accessed on 2 July 2011).

Central Electricity Authority (CEA). 1997. *Fourth National Power Plan, 1997–2012*. New Delhi: Ministry of Power, CEA, Government of India.

Central Electricity Authority (CEA). 2010. *Power Scenario at a Glance*. New Delhi: Ministry of Power, CEA, Government of India.

Chakravarti, Mahadev. 2002. 'Internally Displaced Persons in Tripura: Past and Present', in C.J. Thomas, *Dimensions of Displaced People in North East India*. New Delhi: Regency Publications, pp. 261–73.

Chang, Ha-Joon. 2002. *Kicking Away the Ladder: Development Strategy in Historical Perspective*. London: Anthem Press.

Chin Human Rights Organization. 2004. 'Assessment Report on Burmese Refugees in Mizoram and Delhi', June. Available at http://www.chro.ca/resources/refugee-issues/286-assessment-report-on-burmese-refugees-in-mizoram-and-delhi (accessed on 6 December 2011).

Choudhury, Sujit. 1988. 'Social Background of Mizo Insurgency', mimeo, ICSSR–NERC, Shillong.

Cincotta, Richard P. 2010. 'Demographic Challenges to the State', in Necla Tschirgi, Michael S. Lund, and Francesco Mancini (eds), *Security and Development: Searching for Critical Connections*. Boulder, CO: Lynne Rienner, pp. 77–98.

Collier, Paul. 2007. *The Bottom Billion*. New York: Oxford University Press.

———. 2009. *Wars, Guns, and Votes: Democracy in Dangerous Places*. New York: HarperCollins.

Collier, Paul and Anke Hoeffler. 2004. 'Greed and Grievance in Civil Wars', *Oxford Economic Papers*, 56(4): 563–95.

Collier, Paul, Lani Elliott, Havard Hegre, Anke Hoeffler, Marta Reynal-Querol, and Nicholas Sambanis. 2003. *Breaking the Conflict Trap: Civil War and Development Policy*. Washington, DC: World Bank and Oxford University Press.

Das, Gurudas. 1994. 'Understanding the Underdevelopment of North Eastern Region of India', *Journal of the Anthropological Society*, 29(1 and 2, March/July): 99–104.

———. 1995, *Tribes of Arunachal Pradesh in Transition*. New Delhi: Vikas Publishing House.

———. 1996, 'Migration, Ethnicity and Competition for State Resources: Causes of Social Tension in the North East', in Mehtabuddin Ahmed and Prosenjit Chowdhury (eds), *The Turbulent North East*. New Delhi: Akshar Publications, pp. 121–34.

———. 1997. 'Understanding the Insurgency Phenomenon in India's North-East: An Analytical Framework', in B. Pakem (ed.), *Insurgency in North-East India*. New Delhi: Omsons Publications, pp. 168–96.

———. 1998a. 'Limits to Economic Development of North Eastern Region: An Analysis of Contradictions between Economic Goals and Social Choices', in B. Datta Ray and Prabin Baishya (eds), *Sociological Constraints to Industrial Development in North East India*. New Delhi: Concept Publishing Company, pp. 113–7.

Das, Gurudas. 1998b. 'Social Change and Traditional Tribal Political Systems in Meghalaya', in M.N. Karna, L.S. Gassah, and C.J. Thomas (eds), *Power to People in Meghalaya*. New Delhi: Regency Publications, pp. 32–49.

———. 2000. 'Trade between the North Eastern Region and Neighbouring Countries: Structures and Implications for Development', in Gurudas Das and R.K. Purkayastha (eds), *Border Trade: North-East India and Neighbouring Countries*. New Delhi: Akansha Publishing House, pp. 87–91.

———. 2002a. 'India's North-East Soft Underbelly: Strategic Vulnerability and Security', *Strategic Analysis*, 26(4, October–December): 537–49.

———. 2002b. 'Armed Struggle in Nagaland: Tactics, Strategies and Its Ramifications for Economic Development', in C.J. Thomas and Gurudas Das (eds), *Dimensions of Development in Nagaland*. New Delhi: Regency Publications.

———. 2002c. 'Geo-Economy of Arunachal Pradesh: The Cross-border Trade Dimension', in S. Dutta (ed.), *Cross-border Trade of North East India: The Arunachal Perspective*. Haryana: Hope India Publications, pp. 206–14.

———. 2005a. 'Small Societies in Large Democracy: Problems of Conflict Resolution in India's North East', in Monirul Hussain (ed.), *Coming Out of Violence: Essays on Ethnicity, Conflict Resolution and Peace Process in North East India*. New Delhi: Regency Publications, pp. 39–47.

———. 2005b. 'Sino-Indian Border Trade for Frontier Development: The Case of India's Northeast and China's Southwest', in Jayanta Kumar Ray and Prabir De (eds), *India and China in an Era of Globalization: Essays on Economic Cooperation*. New Delhi: Bookwell, pp. 123–41.

——— (ed.). 2005c. 'Structural Change and Resource-Industry Linkages in India's North East: Some Policy Imperatives', in *Structural Change and Strategy of Development: Resource-Industry Linkages in North East India*. New Delhi: Akansha Publishing House, pp. 327–35.

———. 2006a. 'War and Peace in India's North East: Issues, Complexities and Options', in Prasenjit Biswas and C.J. Thomas (eds), *Peace in India's North East: Meaning, Metaphor and Method*, New Delhi: Regency Publications, pp. 313–38.

———. 2006b. 'Border Trade in India's North-East: Theory and Practice', in David R. Syiemlieh, Anuradha Dutta, and Srinath Baruah (eds), *Challenges of Development in North-East India*, New Delhi: Regency Publications, pp. 332–47.

——— (ed.). 2008a. 'Indo-Bangladesh Relations: Issues in Trade, Transit and Security', in *Indo-Bangladesh Border Trade: Benefiting from Neighbourhood*.

New Delhi Akansha Publishing House, pp. 3–44.

Das Gurudas. 2008b. 'Identity and Underdevelopment: On Conflict and Peace in Assam', in Sujata Dutta Hazarika (ed.), *Peace Dialogue: Universals and Specifics*. New Delhi: Akansha Publishing House, pp. 89–116.

———. 2011. 'Identity, Underdevelopment and Violence: A Roadmap for the Restoration of Peace in North East India', in Gautam Kumar Bera,, Birinchi K. Medhi, R.P. Athparia, and K. Jose S.V.D. (eds), *Social Unrest and Peace Initiatives: Perspectives from North East India*. Guwahati: EBH Publishers, pp. 119–34.

Das, Gurudas and C.J. Thomas. 2005. 'Economy of Myanmar: Trends, Structure and Implications for Border Trade with India's North East', in Gurudas Das, N. Bijoy Singh, and C.J. Thomas (eds), *Indo-Myanmar Border Trade: Status, Problems and Potentials*. New Delhi: Akansha Publishing House, pp. 1–40.

Das, Gurudas and K. Gyanendra Singh. 2007. 'Unemployment in Manipur: Some Policy Implications', in H. Sudhir and Jubita Hajarimayum (eds), *Dimensions of Social Issues in India's North East*. New Delhi: Akansha Publishing House, pp. 89–97.

———. 2009. 'Insurgency and Nationalism in Manipur', *Man and Society*, VI: 51–82.

———. 2010. 'Development of National Peripheries through Mobilizing Cross-Border Synergies: A Case for Sino-Indian Cooperation for the Development of India's Northeast and China's Southwest', in Gurudas Das and C.J. Thomas (eds), *India-China: Trade and Strategy for Frontier Development*. New Delhi: Bookwell, pp. 349–72.

Das, Gurudas and R.K. Purkayastha. 2000. *Border Trade: North East India and Neighbouring Countries*. New Delhi: Akansha Publishing House.

Das, H.N. 2001. 'Insurgency and Development: The Assam Experience', *Faultlines*, no. 10, pp. 59–70.

Dasgupta, Anindita. 2001. 'Human Insecurity and the Threat of Firearms: Perspectives from South Asia: North East India', Background Report for the Small Arms Survey and the Regional Centre for Strategic Studies, Assam.

De, Ranjit Kumar. 1998. *Socio-Political Movements in India*. New Delhi: Mittal Publications.

Debbarma, Khakchang. 2002. 'Internally Displaced Persons in Tripura', in C.J. Thomas (ed.), *Dimensions of Displaced People in North East India*. New Delhi: Regency Publications, pp. 274–81.

Dhar, M.K. 2000. 'The Mekong-Ganga Initiative', *The Sentinel*, 3 December, Guwahati.

Department of Industrial Policy & Promotion (DPIP). 1991–2010. 'Fact Sheet on Foreign Direct Investment (FDI), From August 1991 to September 2010', Ministry of Commerce and Industry. Available at http://www.dipp.nic.in/fdi_statistics/india_fdi_index.htm (accessed on 15 July 2011).

Dixit, J.N. 1998. *Across Borders*. New Delhi: Picus.

———. 2001. 'South Asia's Weak Link', *The Telegraph*, 18 January, Calcutta.

Elwin, Verrier. 1958. *A Philosophy for NEFA*. Shillong: Adviser to the Governor of Assam.

Egreteau, Renaud. 2006. 'Instability at the Gate: India's Troubled Northeast and Its External Connections', CSH Occasional Paper No. 16, Available at www.csh-delhi.com/publications/downloads/ops/OP16.pdf (accessed on 21 January 2010).

Faust, Jorg and Dirk Messner. 2004. 'Europe's New Security Strategy—Challenges for Development Policy', Discussion Paper 3/2004, Deutsches Institut fur Entwicklungspolitik, Bonn.

Godbole, Madhav. 1996. *Unfinished Innings*. New Delhi: Orient Longman.

Gokhale, Nitin. 1998. *The Hot Brew: The Assam Tea Industry's Most Turbulent Decade 1987–97*. Guwahati: Spectrum.

Government of India (GoI). 1948. *Constituent Assembly Debates*, Vol. VII, Appendix C, Annexure–IV, Report of the Sub-Committee on North East Frontier (Assam) Tribal and Excluded Areas, GoI.

———. 2010. *Basic Road Statistics of India, 2004–08*. New Delhi: Ministry of Road Transport and Highways, Transport Research Wing.

Gurr, T.R. 1970. *Why Men Rebel*. Princeton: Princeton University Press.

Haokip, T.T. 2002. 'Ethnic Conflict and Internal Displacement in Manipur', in Joshua C. Thomas, *Dimensions of Displaced People in North East India*. New Delhi: Regency Publications, pp. 221–40.

Hazarika, Sanjoy. 1995. *Strangers of the Mist: Tales of War and Peace from India's Northeast*. New Delhi: Penguin Books India.

The Hindustan Times. 4 April 2001. 'Tehelka Traces Militant Links to Netherlands', *The Hindustan Times*, New Delhi.

Horam, M. 1988. *Naga Insurgency*. New Delhi: Cosmo Publications.

Hout, Wil. 2009. 'Between Development and Security: The European Union, Governance and Fragile States', Paper presented at the 4th GARNET Annual Conference, Rome.

Hussain, Monirul. 1993. *The Assam Movement*. Delhi: Manak.

Hussain, Syed Zarir. 2008. 'Militants in North East Using Drug Money to Buy Arms', 29 April. Available at twocircles.net/node/68146 (accessed on 16 November 2011).

Indian Institute of Entrepreneurship (IIE). 2001. *Prospect of Border Trade with Myanmar and Bangladesh: Pre-Investment Feasibility Report*. Assam: IIE, Guwahati.

Internal Displacement Monitoring Centre (IDMC). 2006. *India: A Profile of the Internal Displacement Situation*. Geneva: Norwegian Refugee Council.

Jain, Purnendra. 2002. 'India's Calculus of Japan's Foreign Policy in Pacific Asia', in Takashi Inoguchi (ed.), *Japan's Asia Policy: Revival and Response*, New York: Palgrave, pp. 211–36.

Jain, Rajeev and J.B. Singh. 2008. 'Trade Pattern in SAARC Countries: Emerging Trends and Issues', Paper presented in SAARC Finance Governors' Symposium, 21 August, Colombo. Also available at http://www.rbi.org.in/scripts/bs_viewcontent.aspx?Id=2255 (accessed on 19 July 2007).

Jana, Jyotirmaya. 2001. 'Andolon aru Matantar' (in Assamese), in Hiren Gohain and Dilip Bora (eds), *Asom Andolon: Pratisruti aru Falasruti*. Guwahati: Banalata, pp. 152–99.

Kar, M. 1990. *Muslims in Assam Politics*. New Delhi: Omsons Publications.

Kaul, Man Mohini. 2001. 'ASEAN-India Relations during the Cold War', in Frederic Grare and Amitabh Matoo (eds), *India and ASEAN: The Politics of Look East Policy*. New Delhi: Manohar, pp. 41–66.

Kumar, Anand. n.d. 'External Influences on the North East Insurgency'. Available at http://fsss.in/agni-volume/2nd/external-influences-on-the-northeast-insurgency.pdf (accessed on 2 July 2011).

Kux, Dennis. 1993. *Estranged Democracies: India and the United States 1941–1991*. New Delhi: Sage Publications.

Kshetri, Rajendra. 2006. *The Emergence of Meitei Nationalism*. New Delhi: Mittal Publications.

Lamb, Alastair. 1960. *Britain and Chinese Central Asia*. London: Pall Mall Press.

Li Peng. 2001. Speech delivered as Chairman, National People's Congress of China, at India International Centre, New Delhi, 13 January 2001 (As published in *The Assam Tribune*, 24 January 2001).

Lintner, Bertil. 1994. *Burma in Revolt: Opium and Insurgency since 1948*. Bangkok: White Lotus.

Lok Sabha Secretariat (LSS). 1997. *Lok Sabha Debates, 11th Series, 5th Session*. New Delhi: LSS.

Mehta, K.L. 1956, 'The Policy of the Government of India for the Administration of NEFA', mimeo, NEFA administration, Shillong.

Mel, Deshal de. 2007. 'South Asia: Towards a Viable Free Trade Area', Briefing Paper No. 5, South Asia Watch on Trade, Economics & Environment (SAWTEE), Kathmandu. Available at www.sawtee.org/publications/Briefing-Paper-16.pdf (accessed on 18 June 2011).

Menkhaus, Kenneth. 2010. 'Beyond the Conflict Trap in Somalia', in Necla Tschirgi, Michael S. Lund, and Francesco Mancini (eds), *Security and*

Development: Searching for Critical Connections. Boulder, CO: Lynne Rienner, pp. 135–70.

Ministry of Defence (MOD). 1993–4. *Annual Report, 1993–4*. New Delhi: MOD, Government of India.

———. 1996–7. *Annual Report, 1996–7*. New Delhi: MOD, Government of India.

———. 1997–8. *Annual Report, 1997–8*. New Delhi: MOD, Government of India.

———. 1999–2000. *Annual Report, 1999–2000*. New Delhi: MOD, Government of India.

———. 1998–9. *Annual Report, 1998–9*. New Delhi: MEA, Government of India.

———. 2007–8. *Annual Report, 2007–8*. New Delhi: MEA, Government of India.

Ministry of Home Affairs (MHA). 1966–7. *Annual Report, 1966–7*. New Delhi: MEA, Government of India.

———. 1970–1. *Annual Report, 1970–1*. New Delhi: MHA, Government of India.

———. 1971–2. *Annual Report, 1971–2*. New Delhi: MHA, Government of India.

Montalvo, Jose G. and Marta Reynal–Querol. 2005. 'Ethnic Polarization, Potential Conflict, and Civil Wars', *The American Economic Review*, 95(3): 796–816.

Murshed, S. Mansoob and Mohammad Zulfan Tadjoeddin. 2007. 'Reappraising the Greed and Grievance Explanations for Violent Internal Conflict', MICROCON Research Working Paper No. 2, Brighton.

Nag, Sajal. 2008. 'Funding the Struggle: Political Economy of Insurgency', in Puspita Das and Namrata Goswami (eds), *India's North East: New Vistas for Peace*, New Delhi: Manas Publications, p. 42.

Naga National Council (NNC). 1993. *The Naga National Rights and Movement*. Kohima, Nagaland: NNC.

Nanda, Prakash. 2003. *Rediscovering Asia: Evolution of India's Look East Policy*. New Delhi: Lancer.

Nehru, Jawaharlal. 1986. *Letters to Chief Ministers, 1947–1964, Vol. 2, 1950–52*, ed. G. Parthasarathi. New Delhi: GoI.

Nehru, Jawaharlal. 1989 (reprint). *Letters to Chief Ministers, 1947–1964, Vol. 3, 1952–54*, ed. G. Parthasarathi. New Delhi: GoI.

Nibedon, Nirmal. 1981. *North East India: The Ethnic Explosion*. New Delhi: Lancer.

North, C. Douglass. 1990. *Institutions, Institutional Change and Economic Performance*. New York: Cambridge University Press.

National Socialist Council of Nagaland (NSCN). 1980. *Free Nagaland, Manifesto*. Nagaland: Oking.

———. 1985. *Polarisation*. Nagaland: Oking.

North Eastern Council (NEC). 2006. *Basis Statistics of North Eastern Region 2006*. Shillong: Ministry of Development of NE Region, GoI. Available at www.indiastat.com (accessed on 28 June 2011).

Parratt, John. 2005. *Wounded Land: Politics and Identity in Modern Manipur*. New Delhi: Mittal Publications.

Phanjoubam, Pradip. 2005. 'Manipur: Revivalist Wave', *South Asia Intelligence Review*, Weekly Assessments and Briefings, 3(41, 25 April). Available at www.satp.org/satporgtp/sair/Archives/3_41.htm (accessed on 10 January 2010).

Pankaj, Prabhat K. 2004. 'Study on Domestic Economic Impact and Social Costs of Adjustment to Alternative Approaches to Liberalization for Bhutan'. Available at http://www.unescap.org/tid/mtg/wtodc_bhu.pdf (accessed on 14 October 2011).

People's Daily Online. 2006. 'India to Invest for the Development of Myanmar Port', 21 December. Available at http://english.peopledaily.com.cn/200612/21/eng20061221_334729.html (accessed on 17 August 2008).

Raju, G.C. Thomas. 1996. *Democracy, Security and Development in India*. New York: St. Martin's Press.

Rammohan, E.N. 2002. 'Manipur: A Degenerated Insurgency', *Faultlines: Writings on Conflict and Resolution, Vol. 11*. New Delhi: The Institute for Conflict Management.

Research and Information System for Developing Countries (RIS). *SAARC Survey of Development and Cooperation, 1998–99*. New Delhi: RIS.

Routray, B. Prasad. 2007a. 'Manipur: The Nexus Again', *South Asia Intelligence Review*, Weekly Assessments and Briefings, 6(14, 15 October). Available at www.satp.org/satporgtp/sair/Archives/6_14.htm (accessed on 11 April 2010).

———. 2007b. 'Manipur: Extortion Rules', *South Asia Intelligence Review*, Weekly Assessments and Briefings, 5(49, 18 June). Available at www.satp.org/satporgtp/sair/Archives/5_49.htm (accessed on 30 April 2010).

Roychoudhury, Prafulla. 1986. *The North East: Roots of Insurgency*. Calcutta: Firma KLM.

Rustomji, N.K. 1973. *Enchanted Frontiers*. Calcutta: Oxford University Press.

Rustomji, N.K. 1983. *Imperilled Frontiers*. Delhi: Oxford University Press.

Sachs, Jeffery D. and Andrew M. Warner. 1995. 'Natural Resource Abundance and Economic Growth', Working Paper No. 5398, National Bureau of Economic Research, Cambridge.

Sahani, Ajai. 2001. 'The Terrorist Economy in India's North East: Preliminary Explorations', *Faultlines*, 8: 127–48.

Sanajaoba, Naorem. 1988. *Manipur: Past and Present, Vol. I*. Delhi: Mittal Publications.

Sen, Amartya. 2006a. *Development as Freedom*. New Delhi: Oxford University Press.

———. 2006b. *Identity and Violence: The Illusion of Destiny*. London: Allen Lane.

Shira, L.D. 1994. 'ALMA Surrender: A Dream Come True', *The Shillong Times*, 11 November, Shillong.

Singh, K. Gyanendra. 2011. *Security & Development: The Political Economy of Insurgency in Manipur*. New Delhi: Akansha Publishing House.

Singh, Swaran. 2010. 'Significance of Nathu La: Border Trade in China–India Relations', in Gurudas Das and C.J. Thomas (eds), *India-China: Trade and Strategy for Frontier Development*. New Delhi: Bookwell, pp. 309–25.

Institute for Defence Studies and Analyses (IDSA). 2004. 'India's Neighbourhood: India and Myanmar', *Strategic Digest*, January. New Delhi: IDSA.

Swaminathan, V.V. 1986. *Problems of Peace and Security in Asia*. New Delhi: Sterling.

Swamy, Subramanian. 2001. *India's China Perspective*. Delhi: Konark Publishers.

Tarapot, Phanjoubam. 1996. *Insurgency Movement in North Eastern India*. New Delhi: Vikas Publishing House.

Tarapot, Phanjoubam. 2005. *Bleeding Manipur*. New Delhi: Har-Anand Publications.

Thapa, Surya Bahadur. 1999. 'The Future of South Asian Cooperation: A Partnership for the Twenty First Century', *South Asian Survey*, 6(2): 173–80.

Thapliyal, Sangeeta. 1999. 'Nepal and Bhutan', in P.R. Chari (ed.), *Perspective on National Security in South Asia*. New Delhi: Manohar, pp. 179–95.

Thakuria, Nava. 2008. 'NISC Criticizes Child Recruitment by Northeast Militants', *News Track*, Tuesday, 26 August, New Delhi.

Tschirgi, Necla, Michael S. Lund, and Francesco Mancini (eds). 2010. *Security and Development: Searching for Critical Connections*. Boulder, CO: Lynne Rienner.

Trivedi, V.R. 1995. *Documents of Assam, Part A*. New Delhi: Omsons Publications.

United Nations Development Programme (UNDP). 2005. *Human Development Report (HDR) 2004, 2005*. New York: UNDP.

Verghese, B.G. 1996. *India's Northeast Resurgent*. Delhi: Konark Publishers.

Weiner, Myron. 1978. *Sons of the Soil*. New Delhi: Oxford University Press.

Weingast, Barry R. 1995. 'The Economic Role of Political Institutions: Market-Preserving Federalism and Economic Development', *Journal of Law, Economics and Organization*, 11(1, April): 1–31.

Weiss, Linda and John M. Hobson. 1995. *States and Economic Development: Comparative Analysis*. Cambridge: Polity Press.

World Bank. 1998. 'The Initiative on Defining, Monitoring and Measuring Social Capital, Social Capital Initiative', Working Paper No. 1, World Bank. Available at http://siteresources.worldbank.org/INTSOCIALCAPITAL/Resources/Social-Capital-Initiative-Working-Paper-Series/SCI-WPS-01.pdf (accessed on 21 June 2011).

———. 2011. *World Development Report: Conflict, Security, and Development*. Washington, DC: World Bank.

Youngs, Richard. 2007. 'Fusing Security and Development: Just another Euro-platitude?' Working Paper No. 43, Fundación para las Relaciones Internacionales y el Diálogo Exterior (FRIDE), Madrid.

Index